Endangered Words

Endangered Words

A Collection of Rare Gems for Word Lovers

Simon Hertnon

SKYHORSE PUBLISHING

Skyhorse Publishing books may be purchased in bulk at special discounts for sales promotion, corporate gifts, fund-raising, or educational purposes. Special editions can also be created to specifications. For details, contact the Special Sales Department, Skyhorse Publishing, 555 Eighth Avenue, Suite 903, New York, NY 10018 or info@skyhorsepublishing.com.

www.skyhorsepublishing.com

10 9 8 7 6 5 4 3 2

Library of Congress Cataloging-in-Publication Data

Hertnon, Simon.
[From afterwit to zemblanity]
Endangered words : a collection of rare gems for word lovers / Simon Hertnon.
p. cm.
Originally published: From afterwit to zemblanity. Auckland : New Holland Publishers, 2008.
Includes bibliographical references and index.
ISBN 978-1-60239-712-5 (alk. paper)
1. Vocabulary. 2. English language--Glossaries, vocabularies, etc. I. Title.
PE1449.H444 2009
428.1--dc22

2009005224
Printed in the United States of America

For J. H. G. and J. S. H.

❧ Acknowledgments

However you look at it, bringing words to life isn't a one-person job.

In addition to acknowledging all of the word lovers whose paths have intersected and enriched my own path to this book, I would particularly like to acknowledge the support and assistance of first, my family, and second, the talented team at New Holland Publishers, New Zealand (and, in particular, Louise for finding and promoting me, and Matt for brilliantly managing the "construction" process). I am indebted to you all.

I would also like to acknowledge: Auckland City Libraries and, particularly, the helpful staff at the Central library (my "office" for the past few months); Dina, Nick and Bryony; the lexicographers and volunteers of the *Oxford English Dictionary*; the contributors to and supporters of Wikipedia (an international treasure if ever there was one).

Lastly, I would like to acknowledge the following people and organizations who have kindly granted permission to reproduce their copyright material:

- ❧ Anton Shammas (concinnity)
- ❧ Penguin Books Ltd, for Bill Bryson (cryptoscopophilia)
- ❧ Reed Business Information, a division of Reed Elsevier Inc., for David Rooney (inamorata)
- ❧ John Alexander (*lagom*)
- ❧ Jennifer Surridge, for Robertson Davies (millihelen)
- ❧ Ray McGovern (nihil obstat)
- ❧ The Random House Group, for Lyndsay Clarke (phrontistery)
- ❧ Pan Macmillan, for Julian Barnes (pluviose)
- ❧ Red Pepper Magazine, for Paul Mason (salariat)

Contents

ॐ Introduction

The seed for this book was planted four years ago. I was reading Bill Bryson's *Mother Tongue* and among its countless treasures I discovered a word (which you will learn in due course) whose unfashionably flaccid meaning quite transfixed me: "a mild desire, a wish or urge too slight to lead to action."[1] The combination of this word's utter relevance, archaic age (around 400 years old) and extreme rarity immediately struck me as something special. I couldn't help but wonder how many other similarly valuable words were languishing out there, in danger of chronic underuse—or oblivion.

Of course, I knew that producing such a list would be as good as impossible—there are just too many English words to consider. (The Second Edition of the *Oxford English Dictionary* [OED] lists some 220,000 distinct English words but the OED editors estimate that, with inflections and technical words included, the total number of English words is likely to be around 750,000.) But it did occur to me that if I were to research the books, web sites and forums of other word investigators then I could, perhaps, compile a dream team of rare lexical gems.

Fast forward three years, opportunity knocked (in the form of the magnificently supportive team from New Holland Publishers), and the journey "from afterwit to zemblanity" began. I really didn't know where it would take me, how long it would take, or how many stops (or dead ends) there would be along the way, but I did know my vocabulary would be hugely enriched and that, most importantly, I would have the precious opportunity to share my discoveries with others.

The 100 selected words are the obvious fruits of my research. Each word stands out but their qualities are far from uniform and, naturally, you will appreciate some more than others. But rather than merely provide you with a list of words and definitions, I have tried to write this book in a manner that enables you to share some of the journey as well.

Before we set off, I wish to clarify the scope of our adventure.

I am not a philologist (an expert in the structure and historical development of language) and this book, though carefully researched, is not a scholarly text. I am a writer and philosopher and my chief motivation is to uncover and promote the value of these 100 special words (and words in general) and all that they tell us about ourselves.

I really do love words and language. I believe words possess a kind of music made up of their sound, shape, etymology, relevance, usefulness and accuracy. When a word perfectly captures a human truth, as with the word from Bryson's book (okay, it's on page 198 if you can't wait), humans respond to it in the same way that they respond to a beautiful melody. They smile. They nod their heads. They tell others of their discovery.

So I have not sought out curiosities or antiquities (though many of the words are both curious and very old); I have sought out words that will make you smile, nod your head, and want to share your discoveries with others.

A GUIDE

The 100 words are listed alphabetically—from afterwit to zemblanity. Each entry features the following:

- Pronunciation guide, type of word, common alternative spellings
- Meaning and related words
- Approximate age (date of first written citation)
- Etymology
- Rarity
- An explanation of why I have chosen the word
- A quotation
- An example of the word used in a modern short story.

At the back of the book you will find an index listing another 150 or so interesting words mentioned throughout the book, and I have also included a list of recommended web sites and books that you can use to further expand your vocabulary.

PRONUNCIATION

The hodgepodge nature of English means that correctly pronouncing unfamiliar words is just a fraction less random than playing darts blindfolded. Accordingly, I have included an unavoidably approximate and intentionally unsophisticated pronunciation guide. The system is:

- syllables are separated with hyphens
- the stressed syllable is capitalized
- if there is a syllable with a secondary stress, it is underlined.

I have used only one phonetic symbol—the upside down "e" (ə) that you will have seen in many dictionaries, which is called a *schwa* (Hebrew for nought), and which stands for the very common *uh* sound of an unstressed syllable. Thus, the word "syllable" would appear as: SIL-ə-bəl.

MEANING

I have relied on three exceptional dictionaries for the word definitions.

I began with my much-thumbed *Random House Dictionary of English*, Second Edition, Unabridged (hereafter referred to as the RH2), which was published in 1987. But I soon realized that I was engaged in a task that required a considerably larger repository of words. Just 48 of the 100 words can be found in the RH2.

So I turned to the Internet and to the online versions of the two heavyweights among English dictionaries: the British *Oxford English Dictionary* (OED) and the American *Webster's Third New International Dictionary*, Unabridged (W3).

The OED's entries are constantly updated and the definitions quoted range in date of publication from 1989 (the year of publication of the 20-volume Second Edition) right up to December 2007. Please note that all post-1989 OED quotations are annotated with the date of the draft entry or revision. An impressive 80 of the 100 words can be found in the online OED.

The W3 was published nearly half a century ago in 1961, but the online version has revisions up to 2002 and contains 67 of the 100 endangered words in this book.

If you are not already familiar with these three dictionaries, you may come to recognize their distinct personalities as our journey progresses. The RH2 is concise and forward-looking, its focus very much on current usage. The OED, on the other hand, has a wholly different character due to its voluntary and extremely valuable role as the repository of English's entire lexicon, including obsolete words.

And the W3 sits in the middle, both in terms of extent and focus.

For the 19 words that do not appear in any of the three main dictionaries,[2] I have turned, in the first instance, to the increasingly reliable duo of Wikipedia (www.wikipedia.org) and Wiktionary (www.wiktionary.org) and, failing that, to absolutely any source I can dig up—all duly cited.

AGE

This is the approximate date of the first recorded usage of the word in an English language publication. For most of the words this date will come from the OED's earliest citation, but for newly coined words or new loanwords that have not yet made it into the OED, the date reflects the earliest usage that I have been able to find.

ETYMOLOGY

The etymologies are intended as useful summaries rather than exhaustive or scholarly histories and, where possible, are composites of the etymologies given by the three dictionaries listed above. Definitions (usually composites from a range of sources, or my own words) are always denoted with quotation marks. And please note that I have used anglicized (scientific) versions of Greek derivations. For example, the Greek **kaloj** appears as *kalos*. Latin words, such as *pandiculātus* appear without the extended final "a"; that is, as *pandiculatus*.

RARITY

Based on current usage data drawn from internet search engine[3] results, I have determined that all 100 featured words are indeed "rare," even when compared with a relatively uncommon word such as "experimentally." For example, the most common word in the list, *chiaroscuro*, is still five times less common than experimentally.

Words denoted as "very rare" are at least 50 times less common than experimentally and words denoted as "extremely rare" are at least 500 times less common.

The rarest word in the list, **elozable**, is around 50,000 times less common than experimentally.

THE WORD ALIVE

To illustrate the word "brought to life," each entry ends with a made-up excerpt containing the word. Put together, these excerpts form an erratic and eclectic short story about Bill and Jane, a fictional couple from London, England. As the character Peter Llewelyn Davies (played so brilliantly by Freddie Highmore) said in *Finding Neverland*, "It's just a bit of silliness, really." But I do hope you enjoy reading it—I certainly had a lot of fun writing it.

afterwit

{AF-tər-wit. Noun; also **after-wit**.}

๛ MEANING

The OED lists four meanings, denoting all but the third as obsolete:

1. Later knowledge, the knowledge of riper years or later times.
2. Second thought, reconsideration.
3. Wisdom after the event, that comes too late.
4. Hence, recognition of former folly, practical repentance, a "coming to one's senses."

So, based on wit being a synonym of knowledge, afterwit is "knowledge gained too late to be of any use." But afterwit has another possible meaning based on wit's later meaning of "repartee." One could describe this kind of afterwit as "a witty remark thought up too late to be used," which is a concept clearly established in the French *esprit de l'escalier* and German *Treppenwitz* (both "wit of the staircase"): witty remarks thought up as one heads down the stairs and out of the house or up the stairs to bed!

The adjective is **afterwitted**.

๛ AGE

Late 16th century

๛ ETYMOLOGY

Afterwit is simply a compound of after and wit.

๛ RARITY

Extremely rare

๛ WHY I LIKE THE WORD AFTERWIT

As a parent of twins, with no other children planned, afterwit perfectly describes a common theme of my parenting experience. Every time my wife and I finally worked out the best way to respond to the latest "phase" (feeding, burping, sleeping, crying, crawling and so on), the phase was over and the next one had begun. Sure, our afterwit is dissipating with every year that passes, but for those frantic first two years (which my wife can only hazily remember) afterwit really was the wit *du jour* in our busy little household.

～AFTERWIT ALIVE

Two weeks ago Jane Mitchell, a successful London interior designer, introduced her attractive but insecure sister Rosamund to her newest client, a rich and handsome Italian dentist named Angelo. At the time she recalled feeling the faintest twitch that she might be making a mistake, that she was unwisely courting **afterwit**, but she knew that this man would appreciate Rosamund's beauty and that this would make Rosamund feel good. And her plan worked, but too well: Rosamund and Angelo were now dating. This had been an undesired outcome, but not a disaster. Seeing, as she just had, Angelo inspecting her nineteen-year-old assistant's gleaming pearly-whites with his tongue, now *that* was a disaster.

agathism

{AG-ə-thiz-əm. Noun.}

ᕫ MEANING
The OED defines agathism as "the doctrine that all things tend towards ultimate good, as distinguished from optimism which holds that all things are now for the best."

ᕫ AGE
Early 19th century

ᕫ ETYMOLOGY
From the Greek *agathos*, "good," and the suffix -ism, which in this case carries the meaning "doctrine."

ᕫ RARITY
Extremely rare

ᕫ WHY I LIKE THE WORD AGATHISM
My interest in philosophy means that I have a healthy appreciation for most "-isms" and the revealing practices, behaviors, and doctrines they describe. But agathism (the word) is new to me and I suspect many people would identify with it, if only they knew it existed.

So, am I an agathist?

I have often been called an optimist (certainly never a pessimist), but I have never felt entirely comfortable with the classification. My love of logic and of common sense makes pragmatist a fit, but not a snug one. And while I am not altogether sure that agathist is a better fit, it does fit. I cannot see how humans could have survived as long as we have if we were not innately inclined to help one another and do "good." Uniquely in the animal kingdom, our capability to screw things up for each other appears to be unlimited, so it follows that it must be our will that keeps that capability in check.

I note the OED's definition makes a distinction between agathism and optimism: one of progression. I like that. I see human life as a relay that I hope will be endless, but I acknowledge this is far from assured.

While researching agathism I also discovered another closely related -ism, meliorism, which the OED (Draft Revision June 2001) defines as "the doctrine that the world, or society, may be improved and suffering alleviated through rightly directed human effort." If this doctrine were a suit, I'm afraid only the pants would fit me because while I have no doubt (but every hope) that we can improve society via more wisely directed actions, the effect of our current population on our environment—"the world"—can only ever be one of degradation. That said, reducing our overall impact would be a stunningly wise place to start.

A meliorist, therefore, I am not. But an agathist? Yes, I probably am.

⟶ AGATHISM ALIVE

Bill Mitchell is a nuclear physicist. Correction. Bill Mitchell *was* a nuclear physicist; now he manages the people who manage nuclear power plants. Bill has just returned from reviewing management performance at three plants in France and the entire trip was a test of his patience, endurance and positivity. But, as is Bill's way, he had remained steadfastly upbeat, his **agathism** shining through. Not even news of Jane's matchmaking would ruin Bill's mood, or so Jane hoped.

ambrosial

{am-BROH-zee-əl. Adjective; also **ambrosiac**, **ambrosian**.}

ᐭ MEANING

In Greek mythology ambrosia (the noun) is, as the OED describes it, "the fabled food of the gods and immortals." To the RH2 it is just plain "food of the gods." The original meaning of the adjective ambrosial is, accordingly: "Belonging to or worthy of the gods, as their food, anointing oil, locks, raiment, sandals, etc." (OED); "worthy of the gods; divine" (RH2).

Figuratively, ambrosial means: "Divinely fragrant; perfumed as with ambrosia; balmy; rarely, Divinely beautiful" (OED); "exceptionally pleasing to taste or smell; especially delicious or fragrant" (RH2). The weather can be ambrosial, so can an island, a forest, a dell.

The OED also defines ambrosial as "celestial, ethereal" and (in a transferred sense) as "belonging to heaven or paradise." It also lists an additional "rare" definition: "Of the pollen of flowers, or of bee-bread."

The adverb is **ambrosially**.

ᐭ AGE

Late 16th century

ᐭ ETYMOLOGY

From the Greek *ambrosios*, meaning "pertaining to the immortals" and, specifically, "the food of the gods," via the Latin *ambrosius*.

ᐭ RARITY

Rare

ᐭ WHY I LIKE THE WORD AMBROSIAL

If, like me, you are an appreciative foodie, then you have probably said something like "mmm, that's delicious" a thousand times. Wouldn't it be nice—just every now and then, when flavor commands—to be able to show your appreciation in a more compelling manner, more compelling than even "mmm, that's *really* delicious."

Wouldn't it be satisfying to be able to "up" the appreciatory (yes, that is a real word) ante without resorting to intensifiers or superlatives? My wife only needs to hear the "mmm" part and she's already cutting me off at the pass: "Yeah honey, I know, it's the best meal you've ever had. That's great."

Seeking an altogether better compliment, I just couldn't go past ambrosial: it's a perfect fit. Sure (as I have since learned), the noun ambrosia has been a tad overused by the brand managers of many food manufacturers, but the adjective is anything but common. Whether people know of this word or not, it is seldom uttered. I am pretty sure I have *never* heard the word used in everyday life.

In these times of unprecedented wealth we are often blessed with meals that are, indeed, fit for the gods. I look forward with anticipation to the next opportunity I have to use this charming word.

⌒ AMBROSIAL ALIVE

Bill loved to cook and, after his long business trip, Jane wasn't surprised to come home to a sumptuous four-course feast. All she had to do was relax and enjoy it—and work out the best moment to tell Bill about Angelo (whom Bill had met and instantly disliked). By the time he served dessert, a creamy millefeuille that she had insensitively called a "custard slice," Jane had decided she would save up her news for another day. Her mind made up, she smiled at Bill, "It was **ambrosial**, dear, you should have been a chef. Now, let *me* do the washing up."

ambsace

{AYM-zays. Noun; also **ambes-ace**, **ambs-ace**, **ame's-ace**, **ames-ace**.}

ᐱᕐ MEANING

As you will see in the etymology section, the literal meaning of ambsace is "both aces," which the OED points out is also the "double ace, the lowest possible throw at dice," though it doesn't mention that the double ace is also called "snake eyes" in North America. Figuratively, ambsace means "bad luck" or "misfortune," as well as "worthlessness, nought, next to nothing."

Ambsace has a third meaning, "the smallest amount or distance" (RH2), based on its use in the phrase "within an ambsace of," a variant of the more common "within an ace of." This phrase is synonymous with many others such as "within a stone's throw" or "within spitting distance."

ᐱᕐ AGE

Late 13th century

ᐱᕐ ETYMOLOGY

Ambsace is a compound of the Latin prefix *amb-*, "both," and ace.

This is a very old word. Middle English writer Geoffrey Chaucer used it more than 600 years ago in the prologue to *The Man of Law's Tale* from his famous and colorful *Canterbury Tales*, at a time when ace was still written in its original form, *as*, from the French: "O noble, o prudent folk, as in this cas! / Your bagges been nat filled with ambes as."[7]

ᐱᕐ RARITY

Extremely rare

ᐱᕐ WHY I LIKE THE WORD AMBSACE

What I love about ambsace is its pessimal quality. Sure, we have enough words to express non-specific optimal qualities (superb, brilliant, fantastic, a cracker, a gem, etc.), but I think we are a little underdone on the other side of the ledger. And let us not forget that ambsace is no "3-out-of-10," "boo-hoo," or "better-luck-next-time" kind of misfortune, it's the worst of the worst. Metaphorically, it is the sediment left *after* you have scraped the bottom of the barrel, and I think it is a helpful and colorful addition to our lexicon.

There is also the fact that other languages have some truly great pessimal words and phrases and we need to make up some ground in this area. Consider the Spanish word *chungo*. Let's say your reportedly wealthy and very generous uncle is coming to stay for a week, this would be *bueno* (good). When the taxi pulls up and Uncle asks you to pay the driver, this would be *malo* (bad). And when you discover that he is penniless and wants to stay until he can "find his feet," this would be *chungo*.

Then there's the Turkish saying, *denize girse kurutur*, which captures the truly pessimal quality of someone for whom deals are always raw and the hands are always rotten. The literal translation is "he gets dry if he enters the sea."[8] Makes me think of Mr. Bean!

❧ AMBSACE ALIVE

Jane was mortified. She had just dropped one of Bill's favorite plates.
"Darling, it doesn't matter," Bill assured her. "It was hardly worth an **ambsace**—I'll just get another one."

anacampserote

{an-nə-KAMP-sə-roht. Noun; also **anacampseros**.}

MEANING

Anacampserote is "a herb feigned to restore departed love" (OED).

Anacampserote doesn't actually appear to be a specific herb. Rather, there are a number of species of the genus *anacampseros* (family: portulacaceae). The etymology of anacampserote is far from extensive, so it is not clear if all or just one of the species of this ancient herb possess this restorative power. The herbs themselves can apparently be found in South Africa, Australia, and the Americas, but they sound pretty rare.

As for anacampserote recipes, I don't think they are that kind of herb.

AGE

Early 17th century

❧ ETYMOLOGY

A French borrowing from the Greek *anakampserös*, formed from *anakamptein*, "to bend back," and *erös*, the Greek god of love, via the Latin *anacampseros*.

Anacampserote is a cognate of the only slightly less rare anacamptic ("causing or suffering reflection; chiefly in reference to sound"[9]).

❧ RARITY

Extremely rare

❧ WHY I LIKE THE WORD ANACAMPSEROTE

The word anacampserote is a bit like a kiwifruit, rough and unappetizing on the outside, but smooth and delicious (perhaps even **ambrosial**) on the inside. I certainly wasn't captured by its awkward sound. No, I was intrigued by its meaning and mesmerized by its etymology: "to bend back love." Oh, that is beautiful: poetic, delicate, hopeful.

On a more practical level, I think the hopeful and positive among the lovelorn could do with a hopeful and positive word to describe their well-intentioned efforts to renew broken relationships. Not everyone who has lost love is obsessed, desperate, needy, or immature. Some just come to the realization that they have made mistakes and are genuinely dedicated to putting things right. To "bend back love"—romantic, platonic, or familial—is no easy task, so my own hope is that this word and its inspiring connotation might aid someone in just such a quest for redemption.

❧ ANACAMPSEROTE ALIVE

As anyone who knows her will tell you, Jane Mitchell is a forthright woman who knows what she wants. Apologies are rare, apologetic expressions are rarer still. The one on her face right at this minute took Bill straight back to the night of his proposal. He had cooked her a reconciliatory meal after a three-month separation. He was so desperate for her to renew her affections for him that he would have used ground-up **anacampserote** in every dish—if only he could have procured some of the stuff.

But he needn't have worried. The diamond engagement ring that she discovered under the strawberry in her champagne cocktail did all the renewing and reinvigorating that was needed.

antepenultimate

{an-tee-peh-NUL-tə-mət. Adjective and noun.}

◯ MEANING

The OED thus defines the adjective: "The last but two. Originally of syllables; but extended to order in place or time." The noun it defines as the syllable itself, presumably "the last but two" syllable which, for antepenultimate, would be the stressed (fourth) syllable.

◯ AGE

Early 18th century

◯ ETYMOLOGY

From the Latin *antepænultimus*, formed from the prefixes *ante-* ("before, in front of ") and *pæne-* (pen-, "almost"), and *ultimus*, ("ultimate, last").

◯ RARITY

Very rare

◯ WHY I LIKE THE WORD ANTEPENULTIMATE

Well, does this word mean "the last but two" (OED) or "before the next to last" (W3) or "third from the end" (RH2) or "two before the last" (Wiktionary) or "the third last" (Wikipedia)?

Clearly, antepenultimate describes a concept that can be described with other words, but it is the only way that you can describe this concept with just a single word. That's tidy. That's accurate. That's my kind of word.

But wait, there's more. Of course, you will already be aware of the single word for "the second last": penultimate. But did you know that there is also a single word for "the fourth last": preantepenultimate? Very cool.

English is an unusually malleable language and this particular feature (adding affixes) is called agglutination. This is not the same as compounding (joining words), which other languages, such as German and Hungarian, are much more accomplished at than English. The (rather tired) poster-boy of English agglutination is antidisestablishmentarianism. Now, I'm not sure I could say that word with a straight face (nor could I think up a reason to utter it), but I think antepenultimate will be a useful addition to my vocabulary and, I hope, to yours too.

༺ ANTEPENULTIMATE ALIVE

In the eight years that Bill and Jane had been married, Bill had learned that the fastest path to Jane's good books was via a box of chocolates, but not just any box of chocolates. Certain brands were okay, others were not okay. And once opened, the chocolates were not "shared." Bill always had to ask for her permission, even if the chocolates had been given by him. And Bill knew he was jeopardizing life and limb taking one of the last chocolates. Obviously, finishing the box was tantamount to declaring war, but even taking the penultimate chocolate was considered to be an act of aggression. Bill was no yellow-belly, but eating the **antepenultimate** chocolate was where he drew the line between risk and reward.

antinomy

{an-TIN-ə-mee. Noun.}

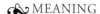 MEANING

The meaning of antinomy is all about contradictions: legal, philosophical and general.

Its legal meaning is, essentially, "a contradiction within a law, or between laws": either way you go to jail! The OED definition also asserts that an antinomy can be "a conflict of authority," though neither the RH2 nor W3 lists this connotation.

The philosophical meaning of antinomy is, according to the RH2, "a contradiction between two statements, both apparently obtained by correct reasoning." The W3 also notes that antinomy is used "*especially*" to denote "a conflict or opposition between the products of reason and of experience."

The W3 defines its general meaning as "an apparent or real opposition, contradiction, conflict, or contrast."

The adjective is **antinomic** and the adverb is **antinomically**.

AGE
Late 16th century

ETYMOLOGY

An adaptation of the Latin *antinomia*, from the Greek, formed from the prefix *anti-*, "against," and *nomos*, "law."

RARITY
Rare

WHY I LIKE THE WORD ANTINOMY

I might be wrong, but I think a good portion of what it is to be human could be described as antinomic. Our very nature is often at odds with itself.

Are any other animals even capable of being self-contradictory?

As I understand things, the behavior of all other animals heads in just the one direction: towards survival. Sure, some very social species, such as monkeys, are clearly adept at having fun and achieving nothing in particular,

but I am pretty certain contradiction never plays a role. They certainly "do
humor" and they might even "do irony," but whatever they chatter about
while they're happily picking fleas off each other, I reckon you can safely bet
the house that "a contradiction within a law" doesn't feature.

No, it is only us humans with our double-edged sword of reason who can
create antinomies and be damned if we do, and damned if we don't.

And I think it is very important to mention that our antinomies are not
confined to the statute books. Like monkeys, we have countless unwritten
laws of interaction: courtship, cohabitation, negotiation, partnership. These
rules are so much more than merely etiquette or good manners and, in our
case, a good share of them are antinomic. I give you just one, painfully real
example: Reduce the mortgage; buy me diamonds.

∽ ANTINOMY ALIVE

The fact that Rosamund lived next door, combined with the fact that
Rosamund and Bill were very close, meant that Jane's ability to keep the
Angelo news hush-hush was limited. But Jane was battling an **antinomy**: the
law of attrition, which dictated that it was highly likely the relationship would
soon peter out; and Murphy's Law, which dictated that Bill would find out
about it before that happened. She told Bill. He wasn't impressed.

antiscian

{an-TEE-shən. Adjective and noun.}

MEANING

The OED tells us that antiscian, the adjective, pertains to "the Antiscii" and, in turn, that antiscii are "those who live on the same meridian, but on the opposite side of the equator, so that their shadows at noon fall in opposite directions."

I currently live in Auckland, New Zealand (approximately 175° E, 37° S) so, for me, an antiscian would be some poor soul stuck on a boat in the middle of the North Pacific Ocean, about 2,000 miles due east of Tokyo.

AGE

Mid-19th century

ETYMOLOGY

Antiscian is the adjectival form of *antiscii*, a Latin word adopted from the Greek *antiskioi*, formed from the prefix *anti-*, in this case meaning "opposite," and *skia*, "shadow."

RARITY

Extremely rare

WHY I LIKE THE WORD ANTISCIAN

As a New Zealander who has spent several years living in Britain, I am very familiar with the term Antipodean, effectively a group noun for Kiwis, Aussies and South Africans.

What I like about antiscian is the "scian" bit—the shadow. I haven't been to either pole and I have difficulty imagining what either looks and feels like (other than very white and very cold), but shadows are real to me, I know their nature, and I did the whole torch-with-a-spinning-globe thing at school and again recently with my own children. So antiscian evokes a mental picture for me: I can see the little people and the shadows and . . . okay, I'll stop with that.

But I won't stop with "scians" because I discovered this word has a couple of very attractive sisters. The older sister (1635) is the plural noun ascians: "Inhabitants of the torrid zone, who twice a year have the sun directly overhead at noon, and then cast no shadows" (OED); from the Greek, *askia*, comprising the prefix *a-*, "without" and *skia*. And the younger sister (1890) is macroscian: "A person whose shadow is long, spec. an inhabitant of the polar regions" (OED); from the Greek, *makros*, "long" and *skia*, perhaps via the French *macroscien*.

ANTISCIAN ALIVE

When Bill arrived home Jane was sitting at the breakfast bar. Her tears were diluting red wine in the bulbous glass over which she was slumped.

She looked up at Bill. "They're moving . . ."

"In together?'

". . . to Malmesbury . . ."

"To Malmesbury?'

". . . South Africa."

"What!'

"*South Africa*, Bill, *South Africa*. Angelo's buying a vineyard or something crazy like that. It could hardly be further away. We'll go from being neighbors to being bloody **antiscians**, for goodness' sake! It's a catastrophe. And it's all my fault."

apophenia

{ə-poh-FEE-nee-ə. Noun.}

✿ MEANING

According to Wikipedia, "Apophenia is the experience of seeing patterns or connections in random or meaningless data. The term was coined in 1958 by Klaus Conrad, who defined it as the 'unmotivated seeing of connections' accompanied by a 'specific experience of an abnormal meaningfulness.'" Klaus Conrad (1905–1961) was an eminent German psychologist.

The adjective is **apophenic**.

✿ AGE

Mid-20th century

✿ ETYMOLOGY

I have seen a suggestion on the popular Languagehat.com[12] web site that this word is derived from the Greek *apophaino*, "to show forth, display." The Greek combining forms *apo-*, "off, away from," and *phaino-* (pheno-) "to show, visible, evident," certainly could add up to being "off the mark with what you see" rather than "to show forth," so it looks as if Conrad adopted the Greek word and adapted its meaning.

The word in Conrad's native German is *Apophänie*.

✿ RARITY

Rare

✿ WHY I LIKE APOPHENIA

Of the 17 entries in this book that have been coined or borrowed within the last 50 years (neologisms and new loanwords), apophenia is easily the most popular. I think the reason for this is very simple: apophenia is part of the human condition—we all do it and we can all identify with it.

If a sentence starts with "*It seems as if...*" then a deeply considered hypothesis could be about to follow, but it is much more likely to be an apophenia. For example: *It seems as if there are more girls than boys being born this year. I know three couples who have all had girls.* Imagine that—all three of them!

There are not suddenly more houses for sale when you happen to be in the market for one. The country isn't necessarily headed for an economic slump just because your sister and your auntie were both layed off last month. And, thankfully, around half of babies born are boys and the other half are girls, regardless of who knows whom.

So are we all idiots because we cannot help but connect dots even when the dots are not actually connected? Absolutely not. Connecting dots is what we do. It is part of the reason we are still here. *Hey Bob, didn't the village flood and half of us drown the last time it rained like this? Just an idea, but maybe we should spend the night up the hill. What do you think?*

Connecting dots is a valuable survival skill and, usually, it doesn't matter if an assumed connection is real or not. But if we consistently express assumptions without any consideration of their logic, we risk a potentially tragic case of cry wolf should we happen to deduce a genuine risk. *The night up the hill, Mary? Come on, you say that every time it rains.*

⌾ APOPHENIA ALIVE

Halfway through the second bottle of Shiraz, Jane had an epiphany. What if she was wrong? It had been dark the night she thought she saw Angelo making out with her assistant. Maybe his flirtatious manner had led her to have a perfectly natural dose of **apophenia** and he really wasn't a smarmy sleazebag after all.

aporia

{ə-POHR-ee-ə. Noun.}

❧ MEANING

The RH2 lists two distinct meanings for aporia:

1. *Rhetoric.* the expression of a simulated or real doubt, as about where to begin or what to do or say.
2. *Logic, Philosophy.* a difficulty encountered in establishing the theoretical truth of a proposition, created by the presence of evidence both for and against it.

The most famous example of aporia's rhetorical meaning is Hamlet's "to be or not to be" soliloquy.

The adjective is **aporetic**.

❧ AGE

Late 16th century

❧ ETYMOLOGY

From the Greek *aporia*, "the state of being at a loss" (adopted from *aporos*, "impassable," which is in turn formed from *a*, "without," and *poros*, "passage"), via Latin.

❧ RARITY

Rare

❧ WHY I LIKE THE WORD APORIA

There is, of course, a significant difference between feigning doubt and being genuinely stumped, but either way the concept interests me.

The former scenario would certainly appear to be the more common. It is, after all, much easier to merely simulate being perplexed than to actually have to go through all of the thinking and reasoning and testing and rethinking that goes with divining truth from conflicting evidence. And simulating perplexion is surely more fun. *Wow. That necklace. The price! Can we afford it? Need to do the numbers. To buy, or not to buy? Gosh, I don't know—so much to think about . . .*

In the scary and bamboozling world of literary deconstruction, aporia can apparently refer to the "point at which a text's self-contradictory meanings can no longer be resolved, or at which the text undermines its own most fundamental presuppositions."[15] Eek! I don't really know what that means but it sounds awful.

∾ APORIA ALIVE

Jane didn't know what to do. Should she tell Rosamund what she had seen? But what if she were wrong? Or should she talk to Angelo? Or should she talk to people who knew Angelo—like the staff at the dental practice that he owned, that she had decorated, but at which he never seemed to actually work? No, what she should do was talk to Bill. He would know what to do.

"Bill, darling, I . . . I just wondered what you . . . I just . . ." She was paralyzed with **aporia** and Bill, as usual, wanted to make her feel better. "A chocolate?" he suggested.

"No. I won't, actually." Bill was stunned. He had known Jane for more than 10 years and never, once, had she turned down a chocolate. "The thing is," she explained, "I think I have a sore tooth coming on. I'll make an appointment. Might even try out Angelo—find out if he's as good as he says he is."

armamentarium

{ahr-mə-men-TAIR-ee-əm. Noun.}

MEANING

For this word, I have chosen to employ the dictionaries' full armamentarium of definitions as it illustrates perfectly the diversity of their scope, focus and style. The OED: "The equipment of medicines, instruments, and appliances used by a medical man. Also *transf.* and *fig.*" The W3 has three definitions:

1. the total store of available resources:
   a : the equipment (as drugs or instruments) and methods used in an activity or profession, especially in medicine
   b : factual, experimental, and speculative data.
2. array (as of materials); collection.
3. essential components; apparatus.

And the RH2 has two:

1. the aggregate of equipment, methods, and techniques available to one for carrying out one's duties.
2. a fruitful source of devices or materials available or used for an undertaking.

So the OED opts for armamentarium's medical pedigree and then covers everything else with just 16 letters—"Also *transf.* and *fig.*"—which means that the word also has transferred senses to contexts outside medicine and is used figuratively. The W3 dryly spells out essentially the same information. And the RH2, as is so often the case, uses carefully chosen words to both sharpen meaning and broaden context, bringing the definitions to life: "the aggregate . . .," "a fruitful source . . . ."

AGE
Late 19th century

❧ QUOTATION ❧

Just as the Patriot Act augmented the government's **armamentarium** against domestic terrorists, the Supreme Court's recent "Guantanamo Bay" decision requires that Congress define procedures to be used against foreign terrorists. These rules must also allow for coercive interrogation, under extremely circumscribed circumstances.

Robert Sklaroff and Michael David Sklaroff,
"Terrorism and 'Torture,'" *The Bulletin*, Philadelphia PA, 18 Aug. 2006

❧ ETYMOLOGY

From the Latin *armamentarium*, "arsenal, armory," from *armamentum*, "armament," from *armare*, "to arm," and the noun-forming suffix, *-mentum*, -ment.

❧ RARITY

Rare

❧ WHY I LIKE THE WORD ARMAMENTARIUM

Armamentarium is a turbocharged word for a toolbox and I love it.

As a writer, I have an armamentarium of vocabulary, conventions, devices and experience that I call on every day to do my job. English itself has its own armamentarium of words, grammar, and usage that we can all probably utilize much more than we do (which, I guess, is what this book is really about). The word is a fitting reminder that English is an extraordinarily well-stocked language and that there is usually a more poignant or compelling word or phrase available than the one that first came to mind, if only you have the time and volition to search for it.

❧ ARMAMENTARIUM ALIVE

The problems at the French plants weren't going away. The increasing demand for nuclear power was creating growing pains that needed to be addressed at every level and Bill needed a plan—a big plan. To be successful Bill would need to call upon his entire **armamentarium** of skills, experience, and relationships. And he would also need help. It was time to promote someone.

arriviste

{ah-ree-veest. Noun; also **arrivist**.}

ᔷ MEANING

This is a colorful and dynamic borrowing from French that essentially means "ambitious upstart," but my three dictionaries certainly don't agree on the degree of ignominy attached to the label.

The OED is the most generous, defining an arriviste as "one who is bent on 'arriving,' i.e., on making a good position for himself in the world; a pushing or ambitious person, a self-seeker."

The RH2 is less generous: "a person who has recently acquired unaccustomed status, wealth, or success, especially by dubious means and without earning concomitant esteem."

And there is no generosity whatsoever in the W3's: "one who employs any means however questionable or unscrupulous to achieve success: an aggressive pushing person: parvenu, upstart." To rub salt into the wound, the W3 illustrates its definition with this pithy instructional quotation: "an impoverished family of high breeding and training sneers self-consolingly at vulgar *arrivistes*—John Hersey."

The abstract noun, describing the conduct or condition of an arriviste, is **arrivism**.

ᔷ AGE

Early 20th century

ᔷ ETYMOLOGY

Arriviste is a loanword from French, formed from *arriver*, "to arrive," and *-iste*, -ist.

ᔷ RARITY

Very rare

ᔷ WHY I LIKE THE WORD ARRIVISTE

What's not to love about the phrase "one who is bent on 'arriving'"? Is that bent out of shape? Bent over? Bent backwards? And those quotation marks around arriving: with consummate efficiency they compel you to pause and really emphasize "arriving." "Arriving" (with the inverted commas) is clearly nothing like just plain arriving. And while I have no doubt that there are countless upstarts, careerists, go-getters and the like, not everyone who is ambitious can actually make an impact with an entrance, either a physical one or a metaphorical one.

So successful arrivistes perhaps deserve a little more respect than that offered by their label, should it linger. Though, I guess it is more likely that they will simply be reclassified as parvenus or nouveaux riches.

And for the unsuccessful arrivistes? It will come as no surprise that we have borrowed yet another word from French for this: manqué (an adjective). The idea here is that you just take the arriviste's unrealized profession (say, actor) and add manqué to form an actor manqué, "someone who might have been an actor but, through their own failing, isn't." Ouch.

But however things work out for arrivistes, I think it should be pointed out that the strongly motivated are usually much more interesting folk than those who just muddle along.

❧ ARRIVISTE ALIVE

The obvious person for Bill to promote was Jerry Johnson. Jerry was a tall and charismatic Canadian who was highly capable but suffered from one small but significant flaw: He tried too hard. His compliments flowed just a touch too easily, his offers of assistance were always just a touch too eager. He was ambitious—an **arriviste** even—and when Bill really thought about the challenges ahead he realized that Jerry's undeflatable enthusiasm was exactly what he would need.

astrobleme

{ASS-trə-bleem. Noun.}

❧ MEANING

An astrobleme is "a scar on the earth's crust made by the impact of a meteorite" (W3). Unlike a crater, an astrobleme doesn't necessarily need to be cup-shaped, so it is a useful word. But, for a reason that is not apparent (at least, not to me), the OED does not list the word.

This *is* unusual—we are not in **apophenia** territory here. Of my 100 words, astrobleme is the only one that isn't listed in the OED but is listed in either the W3 or the RH2 (it is listed in both). It can also be found in Wikipedia, the *Britannica Online Encyclopedia, The American Heritage Dictionary of the English Language* (Fourth Edition, 2000), and a wide range of other publications.

According to the RH2 the word was coined between 1965 and 1970, so the OED's usual five-year probationary period should have long passed. And we know the astro- prefix is familiar to the OED editors: "astrobolism: *Medical. Obsolete.* Sudden paralysis attributed to the malign influence of a planet or star; sunstroke; blasting of plants in the dog-days."

It's all very odd.

❧ AGE

Late 20th century

❧ ETYMOLOGY

Formed from the prefix astro- (from the Greek *astron*, "star"), and -bleme (from the Greek *blëma*, "missile, wound").

❧ RARITY

Very rare

❧ WHY I LIKE THE WORD ASTROBLEME

As illustrated in the quotation opposite, the alternative term for astrobleme is "impact structure." Hmm. Astrobleme certainly sounds a great deal more exotic to my ears.

And an astrobleme *is* exotic. A "star missile" from space, the final frontier (no, I'm not a Trekkie, but I do adore *The Hitchhiker's Guide to the Galaxy* and can quote one or two passages from it with unnerving ease), crashing into Earth, wreaking havoc, and marking its powerful, destructive path with a massive "star wound." Impact structure can't compete with that.

Astrobleme is also a poetic word. A "star wound" conjures up all manner of creative imagery whereas impact structure conjures up nothing at all. In fact, if words were geographical locations, astrobleme would be in the middle of a teeming and vibrant jungle while "impact structure" would be in, well, Milton Keynes. On a Sunday. Morning. Early.

At the risk of drifting even further off track, I want to mention that astrobleme reminds me of this fantastic word . . . that I can't for the life of me remember, and which may, in fact, not actually exist. But I *think* there is a word, or phrase, possibly French, that means "heart wound"—a figurative scar on the heart, the kind you might find on an **anacampserote**-hunting ex. If there isn't such a word, we need to make one up; heart-broken is such a cliché. And, yes, I have already ruled out "cardiobleme."

☙ ASTROBLEME ALIVE

Jane wasn't remotely surprised to learn that Angelo's staff saw him as a rich playboy, a smooth businessman, and a modestly skilled dentist, in that order. And now this man wanted to take her sister to the other side of the planet. Rosamund and Jane were extraordinarily close and Rosamund's departure would leave a scar on the landscape of Jane's life like a giant **astrobleme**.

ataraxia

{AT-ə-rak-see-ə. Noun; also **ataraxy**.}

ᐱ MEANING

Ataraxia is "freedom from disturbance of mind or passion; stoical indifference" (OED) or, as the W3 puts it (more poetically): "Calmness untroubled by emotional disquiet: intellectual detachment, imperturbability."

Both the OED and W3 actually list ataraxy as their main entry, with ataraxia as a variant, but I have opted for the significantly more popular ataraxia, as did the RH2. Its definition: "a state of freedom from emotional disturbance and anxiety; tranquillity."

The adjective is **ataraxic** or **ataractic**.

ᐱ AGE

Early 17th century

ᐱ ETYMOLOGY

From the Greek *ataraxia*, "impassiveness," formed from *a*, "without" and *tarrasein*, "to disturb, stir up," possibly via the French *ataraxie*.

ᐱ RARITY

Rare

ᐱ WHY I LIKE THE WORD ATARAXIA

In a society being shaken apart by its own overcomplicated busyness, mental calmness is a rare and restorative condition. If one thinks of ataraxia as tranquillity (or "peace of mind" as I have seen it informally, and perhaps hopefully, defined), achieving it may eventually become more highly prized than even our most popular contemporary obsessions: possessions and status.

But ataraxia is not synonymous with nirvana, and I would far rather live a turbulent life in a slower, more discerning world than an ataraxic (and, presumably, isolated) life within the current frenzy.

Ataraxia is one of around ten "Stoic concepts" (including eudaimonia, "well-being, happiness") that support the stoic philosophy. Essentially, Stoicism teaches that clear and logical thinking allows you to understand the way the world works, thus enabling you to avoid much of the "emotional disquiet" of life by being able to confidently distinguish what matters from what doesn't. For example, another stoic concept, adiaphora, teaches that some things just don't matter—they are "neutral"—which helps to combat the natural human tendency to blow things out of proportion, thus artificially making events and, through association, our lives, more important. The downside of this is that we never get to relax. Sound familiar? Oh, those ancient philosophers knew a thing or two!

❧ ATARAXIA ALIVE

Jane could understand Rosamund's falling for Angelo—his charms were there for all to see—but what she couldn't understand was Rosamund's **ataraxia** in the face of all the changes that were about to happen: the move, and their separation from each other. Or did Jane just not know her sister as well as she thought she did?

ballicatter

{BAH-lee-cət-er. Noun; also **ballacader**.}

❧ MEANING

Ballicatter is a regional word from Newfoundland, Canada, so I needed to find a regional dictionary and, courtesy of the Memorial University's *Heritage* web site, I did.

The Dictionary of Newfoundland English (Second Edition, 1999) thus defines ballicatter:[18]

1. Ice formed by the action in winter of spray and waves along the shore-line, making a fringe or band on the landward side.
2. A narrow band of ice formed in winter in the salt water along the foreshore or "landwash"; shore: ~ ice; large slabs, chunks and fragments of this ice after break-up.
3. A floating ice-pan.
4. Frozen moisture around the nose and mouth.

Or, as defined by MSN Encarta, ballicatter is simply "a ridge of ice formed along a shoreline by waves and freezing spray."[19]

❧ AGE
Early 19th century

❧ ETYMOLOGY

The etymology of ballicatter is something of a mystery. *The Dictionary of Newfoundland English* offers no clues and MSN Encarta offers just one, "alteration of barricade," without reference.

Dead ends are, of course, invitations to look elsewhere, so that's exactly what I did.

I knew that bally used to be a euphemism for the intensifier "bloody," as in, *I say old chum, it's bally cold out here in this icy spray.* So, that could fit. But what of "catter"?

Given the context, if I told you that catter is a variant of a word relating to cold, would you just shrug that off as a coincidence? No bally way! Catarrh, of which catter is a Scottish variant, means: "The profuse discharge from nose and eyes which generally accompanies a cold" (OED). Okay, it's *a* cold, not *the* cold, which slightly weakens the link, but look again at the fourth definition opposite. And isn't Newfoundland next to Nova Scotia? My imagination can certainly connect all of these dots. Surely it's not **apophenia**!

～ RARITY
Extremely rare

～ WHY I LIKE THE WORD BALLICATTER
In my notes for this book I had three words next to ballicatter: regional, poetic, visual. But I think now that, as with **astrobleme**, it was the word's exoticism that fixed my interest (the etymology adventure came much later).

I have lived (mainly) in the temperate climate of the North Island of New Zealand. To see snow I have to go to a mountain. To see more than a cube of ice I have to go to an ice rink. I have never seen ballicatter. To me, it is exotic because imagining it means imagining myself in the kind of location where it can exist, and that implies having embarked on an expedition. Nature and travel. Bally exciting, I say, what!

～ BALLICATTER ALIVE
Someone had to go to the nuclear-waste facility on Nova Zembla, a desolate island north of Russia in the freezing Arctic Ocean, and Bill knew just the man for the job. Keen to make every post a winner, Jerry didn't protest one bit. And when he arrived at Nova Zembla, he even reported back cheerfully that the **ballicatter** was "just like the ballicatter at home."

bleezed

{BLEEZD. Adjective; also **bleezy**.}

ᢙ MEANING

As an adjective, bleezed appears in the OED's entry for bleezy: "*Scottish*. Affected in the eyes, as by alcoholic excitement. Jamieson has also *Bleezed*, explained as 'a little flustered.'" The "Jamieson" reference is to the dictionary, *An Etymological Dictionary of the Scottish Language* (1808),[20] by the Reverend John Jamieson, a Scottish lexicographer.

I believe the OED is referring to a version of Jamieson's dictionary that was revised between 1879 and 1887, but I could only manage to locate two earlier revisions: an abridged version by John Johnston (1846) and an enlarged version (of the abridged version) by John Longmuir (1867).[21] The latter defined bleezed as signifying "the state of one on whom intoxicating liquor begins to operate" and noted that "it especially denotes the change produced in the expression of the countenance; as, *He looked bleezed-like.*"

Put simply, then, bleezed is a synonym for drunk.

ᢙ AGE

Early 19th century

ᢙ ETYMOLOGY

The OED suggests bleezed is derived from bleezy, which is in turn derived from bleeze (the verb), which it defines as the Scottish dialectical variant of blaze (both in terms of its common meanings, "to burn, light a fire, shine," and of a rarer meaning, "to declaim, talk loudly").

However, in the Longmuir version of Jamieson's dictionary, a different etymology is suggested: "Perhaps *bleezed* . . . is allied to Fr. *blas-er*." This is the French verb, *blaser*, "to make blasé, to be indifferent." Completing the circle (real or **apophenic**), blasé is defined by the OED as "exhausted by enjoyment," which could certainly describe the condition of someone at the end of a long session of drinking.

ᢙ RARITY

Very rare

⌒QUOTATION⌒

Some greybeard came knocking
and mama settled him square off to the beggar's bed
in our cowshed

He beared to be a trifle **bleezed**
making some face that was meaning to sneeze
I expected he'd be alright . . .

Kimmy Van Kooten,
excerpt from "Back to Dead," AuthorsDen, 15 Sept. 2007[22]

❧ WHY I LIKE THE WORD BLEEZED

If you are thinking that there are probably already dozens of synonyms for drunk, and that this book is supposed to be about words we actually need, words with unique meanings, then you would be wrong and right, in that order.

There are not dozens of synonyms for drunk; there are thousands (no exaggeration). Bleezed, therefore, is not just an exception to the rule of unique words, it is, specifically, its antithesis.

This is our cue for a wee side-trip, a *divertissement*, into the world of the premier English language "synonymist" Paul Dickson. In 1982 Dickson published a book called *Words* and in it he listed 2231 synonyms for drunk. I had to see this list for myself so I tracked down a copy of his later (1992) book, *Dickson's Word Treasury*,[23] in which the list had grown to an astonishing 2600. Just a few of my favorites: antifreezed, embalmed, irrigated, Kentucky-fried, lit up like Main Street, off to Mexico, skew-whiff, and wallpapered (a variant of the more common "plastered"). Bravo, Mr. Dickson.

BLEEZED ALIVE

Bill decided it would be a prudent move to call Forbes, the Scottish foreman on Nova Zembla, to check up on Jerry.

"Aye, Bill, ye've nothing to worry about. He's a good lad, though he's looking a little **bleezed** the noo—local vodka, ye ken the story. Och, but he brought a pharmacy of pills with him so he's bound to have something for a hangover."

caliginous

{kə-LIJ-ə-nəs. Adjective.}

ᐡ MEANING

One never expects absolute agreement between dictionaries, so these definitions are unusually concurrent.

OED: Misty, dim, murky; obscure, dark; also figuratively.

RH2: Misty; dim; dark.

W3: Misty; dark; obscure.

The noun is **caliginosity** or **caliginousness**. The adverb is **caliginously**.

ᐡ AGE

Mid-16th century

ᐡ ETYMOLOGY

From the Latin *caliginosus*, "misty," formed from *caligo, caligin-is*, "mistiness, obscurity."

ᐡ RARITY

Very rare

ᐡ WHY I LIKE THE WORD CALIGINOUS

This is the first of two adjectives (the other is **delitescent**) that I have chosen because they seem to me to occupy unique semantic real estate: We need these words.

The light can be dim and dark, but not murky. Air can be murky, but not dim or dark. A view can be obscure, but not dim, dark or murky. A room can be dark (a dark room, not a darkroom) but not obscure; it can be dimly lit, and it can contain murky or misty air, but it cannot itself be dim, murky or misty. But an alleyway (or a hallway, or a nook, or the corner of a room) can *appear* caliginous: dark, dim, murky, misty; all combining to make it obscure to the observer.

What else can be caliginous?

Thoughts can be obscure, but not misty or murky. They can be dark, but that is something quite different from thoughts that are dim. But caliginous thoughts are not "misty, dim, murky; obscure [or] dark": they are caliginous—a unique combination (to each context, to each observer) of all those qualities. I know that I have had caliginous thoughts and I suspect every human has, at one time or another. Are you nodding?

Caliginous is like a tried and tested recipe that perfectly combines certain aspects of its ingredients. It is not synonymous with any one of the ingredients; it has its own distinctive flavor.

❦ CALIGINOUS ALIVE

Rosamund's impending departure caused Jane's mood to be **caliginous**, but this changed the instant Jane learned that the South African "deal" had fallen through. Jane cried and then swore with relief. But that wasn't all of Rosamund's news. They were now going to live in Chicago where Angelo would be opening a new clinic. And they were leaving in a week's time.

charientism

{kə-ree-EN-tiz-əm. Noun.}

๏ MEANING

The OED refers to its citations for the definition of this obsolete but unquestionably relevant noun: "1709 *Brit. Apollo* II. No. 19. 1/1 A Charientism is that Species of an Irony, which couches a Disagreeable Sense under Agreeable Expressions."

Wiktionary, quoting from the *Cyclopedia* (1728), defines charientism as: "(*rhetoric*) A figure of speech wherein a taunting expression is softened by a jest; an insult veiled in grace."

๏ AGE

Late 16th century

๏ ETYMOLOGY

From the Greek *charientismos*, "gracefulness of style, expression of an unpleasant thing in an agreeable manner," via the Latin *charientismus*.

๏ RARITY

Extremely rare

๏ WHY I LIKE THE WORD CHARIENTISM

Before discussing my newfound interest in gracefully veiled insults, I want to first establish my interest in clever insults, regardless of their style of delivery.

My wife, a naturally competitive person, often remarks at my lack of competitiveness (despite my being a keen sportsman). But I assure you there is one element of sport at which I am highly motivated to win and not just compete: talking smack.

My favorite example of cleverly traded insults is from the famous political and personal rivalry between the 19th-century British political opponents, Benjamin Disraeli and William Gladstone. At a social gathering Gladstone chided Disraeli with, "I predict, sir, that you will die either by hanging or of some vile disease." Disraeli replied, "That all depends, sir, upon whether I embrace your principles or your mistress."

But this wonderful example is not a charientism, which is a below-the-radar, sugar-coated kind of insult. The key characteristic seems to me to be that the insulted remains blissfully unaware of the insult, despite it being delivered openly and directly. Depending on the circumstances, a simple phrase like *"that dress is really flattering"* could do the trick. Alternatively, a superior vocabulary will always provide a range of charientism opportunities, where the insultee simply fails to recognize the jibe. The word **arriviste**, for example, could come in handy. Or you might get some mileage out of our next word, **chavish** (I know I will), or perhaps *Drachenfutter* will prove useful. **Elozable** will certainly help, and then there's **lalochezia**, **nikhedonia**, **peccable**, **plutomania**, *Schlimmbesserung*, **sprezzatura**, **tu quoque**, **velliety**, **verbigerate,** and **zemblanity**. But remember, charientisms need to be graceful and "agreeable"—no easy task. The last thing I want to encourage is boorish language.

∽ CHARIENTISM ALIVE

The week rushed by in a blink and a departure gate beckoned the dashing couple. Jane couldn't resist a farewell **charientism** for her former client: "My dear Angelo, we shall all miss you so much. Particularly my impressionable young assistant who, I think, was really quite taken by your irresistible charm."

chavish

{CHAY-vish. Noun.}

᏶ MEANING

According to the Reverend W. D. Parish's *A Dictionary of the Sussex Dialect* (Farncombe & Co., 1875),[26] a chavish is "a chattering or prattling noise of many persons speaking together. A noise made by a flock of birds." And this is the definition of the word that both the OED and W3 list. However, many readers will be aware of the recent and rapid emergence of a heteronym (a word pronounced differently but spelt the same as another) pronounced with a short "a" (CHAV-ish).

This other chavish is an adjective pertaining to the noun, chav, which the OED (Draft Entry June 2006) defines thus: "In the United Kingdom (originally the south of England): a young person of a type characterized by brash and loutish behavior and the wearing of designer-style clothes (esp. sportswear); usually with connotations of a low social status."

᏶ AGE

Late 17th century

᏶ ETYMOLOGY

Who knows? The OED offers nothing but an invitation to compare chirm; the W3 offers "probably imitative"; and chavish isn't listed in the RH2.

I looked up chirm (the noun) in the OED:

1. Noise, din, chatter, vocal noise (in later times esp. of birds).
2. Especially, the mingled din or noise of many birds or voices, the "hum" of school children, insects, etc.
3. A company or flock (of finches). *Obs.*

It certainly sounds familiar, but does it help us determine the etymology of chavish (the elder)? I think not. The verb chavel appears more closely related ("to wag the jaws; to chatter, talk idly"), but I am really just clutching at straws.

So let us turn our attention to chavish (the younger) and to what Alex Games gleefully described in *Balderdash & Piffle* (BBC Books, 2006) as the "huge debate in linguistic circles" about the origin of its root, the humble chav. Option one, Games summarizes, is "that it comes from the Chatham area of Kent, where a lot of chavs live and don't exactly work." That would make chav a toponym (a word named after a place), and a pretty unusual one at that given the shortened form and non-standard pronunciation. Option two is that it "comes from the Romany *chavi*, meaning "child." The establishment (that is, the OED) mentions both etymologies but clearly favors the Romany one, concluding that the Chatham "suggestion" is "prob. a later rationalization."

~ RARITY

Extremely rare

~ WHY I LIKE THE WORD CHAVISH

Have you ever asked yourself the question: if you had to lose either your hearing or your sight, which would you choose? It is a very interesting and illuminating question. My choice would be to retain my hearing—no contest—but my wife would choose the opposite. I have sensitive hearing and a primal love of music. I have an ear for accents. I cannot imagine life without sound. And, of course, I love words and good conversation.

Put all this together and you can understand why chavish, the word and the sound it describes, interests me. I enjoy the informality of its unstructured, but patterned, ebb and flow. I enjoy deciphering the accents and conversations it comprises. And I can be driven round the bend by it if the conversation is inane and I am an unwilling participant *sans* an exit strategy.

~ CHAVISH ALIVE

Jane couldn't hear herself think over the **chavish** of the airport departure hall, but Bill could still hear Jane's rib-shaking sobs. His wife was inconsolable and he had to accept that there was nothing he could do. He found that terribly hard.

chiaroscuro

{kee-ahr-oh-SKYOOR-oh. Noun and adjective.}

MEANING

This is a word whose literal meaning, "light-dark," describes a sufficiently universal quality for it to be applied to a wide range of "things": style, method, treatment, effect, sketch, print.

A chiaroscuro can be a black-and-white sketch or a woodcut print.

As a pictorial style, chiaroscuro is "representation in terms of light and shade without regard for or use of colors in the objects depicted; *specifically:* drawing or painting in black and white" (W3). It can also apply to photography and cinematography.

Chiaroscuro also describes the method, or treatment, used to create such art. And the effect of "the use of marked light and shade contrasts" can stem from the "interplay of light and shadow," dramatically highlighting "mood, style, character, or spirit" (W3).

Figuratively, chiaroscuro can be "used of poetic or literary treatment, criticism, mental complexion, etc., in various obvious senses, as mingled "clearness and obscurity," "cheerfulness and gloom," "praise and blame," etc." (OED).

AGE

Late 17th century

ETYMOLOGY

Chiaroscuro is a loanword from Italian, comprising *chiaro*, "light, bright" (from the Latin *clarus*), and *oscuro*, "dark" (from the Latin *obscurus*).

RARITY

Rare

WHY I LIKE THE WORD CHIAROSCURO

First and least importantly, the next time I am in an art gallery I will now be able to make at least one knowledgeable-sounding comment: this is a significant achievement for me.

Second, I love the art style. It's the same with black-and-white photography—I find the lack of color leaves more room for viewers to add their own meaning and emotion. If you visit the chiaroscuro page on Wikipedia, you will see some stunning examples.

Third, I love the sound of the word. The Italian language is music to my ears and I hope one day to learn and actually converse in it. (It's on my to-do list, you know the deal!)

Fourth (and last), I love the word's figurative capabilities, both as a noun and as an adjective. The OED mentions the figurative meaning: "partly revealed and partly veiled." This could apply to a face, a neck, a plan, a motive, even an identity. *A chiaroscuro hero.*

✑ CHIAROSCURO ALIVE

For the next month, Jane's view of the world was like a 17th-century Dutch **chiaroscuro** painting—almost all dark but with a few pockets of light that immediately drew your eye or, at least, Bill's eye. He knew there was nothing he could say that would stop Jane from missing her sister so he just gave her the only helpful things he could—time and space.

concinnity

{kon-SI-nə-tee. Noun.}

❧ MEANING

Our dictionaries agree that concinnity is some kind of "skillful and harmonious adaption or fitting together of parts" (OED), but whether it relates specifically to rhetoric (RH2), literary style (W3 and OED), artistic style or music (both OED) is unclear and probably unimportant.

Both the OED and W3 mention "studied elegance" and, whatever the context, that sure sounds like a fine thing.

The adjective is **concinnous** and the verb is **concinnate**.

❧ AGE

Early 16th century

❧ ETYMOLOGY

From the Latin *concinnitas*, formed from *concinnus*, "skilfully put together," and *-itas*, -ity.

❧ RARITY

Very rare

❧ WHY I LIKE THE WORD CONCINNITY

I might as well just say that I am completely charmed by this word. I deeply appreciate artistic skill and I deeply appreciate harmony of design in all its forms. A word to describe their profitable combination is a lexical treasure.

I can think of concinnous music, concinnous plays, concinnous novels, concinnous movies, concinnous bridges, concinnous churches, concinnous yachts, concinnous watches, concinnous outfits, concinnous partnerships and concinnous events.

And, of course, the counterpoint to all this concinnity is inconcinnity: "Want of concinnity, congruousness, or proportion; inelegance, awkwardness; impropriety, unsuitableness" (OED).

We all need to know about these words because the concepts they describe are integral to the very quality and, ultimately, viability of our lives. If we relearn how to create concinnous communities, despite all the temptations of just doing new stuff, we may be able to prosper again. But if we continue to fête the concinnity of an iPod while completely ignoring the inconcinnity of almost every aspect of the economic culture that delivered it to us, we will surely become unstuck, and our children will be left to deal with the many deficits we are so busily creating.

☙ CONCINNITY ALIVE

Bill threw himself into his work with unexpectedly positive results. It turned out that Jerry Johnson was even more talented than Bill knew. Jerry played chess, properly. He was one of those rare people who could think several moves ahead and not get lost. This skill, combined with Bill's empathy for the core change-management issues facing their company, had resulted in their creating a program whose **concinnity** might just open hearts and minds. They were fast becoming the "Bill and Jerry Team." Yes, they both liked the sound of that.

concupiscible

{kon-KYOO-pis-sə-bəl. Adjective.}

◌ MEANING

The RH2 defines concupiscible as "worthy of being desired," which sounds rather limp when compared to the OED's "vehemently desirous."

In scholastic philosophy, concupiscible (which describes the innate desire for good) is the partner to irascible (which describes the innate courage and aggression sometimes needed to attain that which you desire).

The noun is **concupiscence**, which the OED defines as "eager or vehement desire" which, in theological terms, translates to "the coveting of "carnal things," desire for the "things of the world." It also lists a second meaning: "libidinous desire, sexual appetite, lust."

◌ AGE

Late 15th century

◌ ETYMOLOGY

Adapted, via French, from the Latin *concupiscibil-is*, formed from *concupiscere*, "to desire strongly," which is in turn formed from the prefix *con-*, "with," and the verb *cupere*, "to desire."

◌ RARITY

Very rare

◌ WHY I LIKE THE WORD CONCUPISCIBLE

How does one go past "vehemently desirous"? We want so much these days—things we may or may not need, deserve or even understand—that surely our desires can at best be described as "thinly spread"—much like Professor Shammas's metaphorical pita (see **concinnity**).

When I was a child the anticipation that built up for my "main" Christmas present was positively concupiscible. Relative to the other presents (usually paperbacks or chocolate bars), this present was a big deal. As I grew older, I started contributing to the cost of this present so that it could be even more significant, which of course made me desire it even more vehemently. And where did that money come from? I earned it delivering newspapers, selling fruit, mopping floors—all useful roles that were sufficiently dull to force me to fill my mind with the imagined joys of spending *my* money.

Today, I have concupiscible passions for few material possessions, but a whole catalogue of experiences (travel, food, fun, relaxation—all the good things in life). And there is one last concupiscible passion (of the lustful variety, to be sure) that I should mention: the one for my gorgeous wife.

❧ CONCUPISCIBLE ALIVE

Slowly, Jane's depression lifted, buoyed no doubt by the undeniable fact that things could have been worse. If she really needed to see Rosamund, she could be in Chicago within a day. This morning, Bill could see evidence of this shift in mood in her choice of dress and her body language. To Bill, Jane was always a **concupiscible** woman, but seeing her go through this difficult period only served to remind him how much he loved her.

cryptoscopophilia

{krip-toh-skoh-pə-FIL-ee-ə. Noun.}

MEANING

This raunchy neologism doesn't yet appear in the OED, but you may well be able to deduce its meaning from its more common components: the combining form crypto- and the word scopophilia.

Crypto- is derived from the Greek *kryptos* and means "hidden" or "secret." The OED defines scopophilia as "sexual stimulation or satisfaction derived principally from looking; voyeurism."

Put the two together, as Bill Bryson did in *Mother Tongue*—his highly entertaining tour of the vagaries of English—and you will end up with what at least six online sex dictionaries have all defined (word-for-word) as "desire to see behavior of others in privacy of their home, not necessarily sexual."

I prefer Bill's definition (see the quotation) and, yes, I suppose I am a **cryptoscopophiliac**. Aren't we all?

AGE
Late 20th century

ETYMOLOGY

I have no idea who coined this term but, as I have mentioned above, it is obviously formed from the prefix crypto- and the word scopophilia. Scopophilia is in turn formed from scopo- (from the Greek *skopia*, "observation") and the Greek combining form *-philia*, "love of or liking for."

It is interesting to note that Bill incorrectly spelt cryptoscopophilia and, in all likelihood, as a direct result of this there are now nearly as many instances on the Internet of his misspelling as of the correct spelling. This is how many of our words and names have evolved. My own "extremely rare" last name, Hertnon, is almost certainly the product of a lengthy series of misspellings of the much more common Irish surname, Heffernan.

RARITY
Extremely rare

❧ WHY I LIKE THE WORD CRYPTOSCOPOPHILIA

This is a word whose usage, I predict, will only grow. As with **apophenia**, cryptoscopophilia accurately describes a human trait, so people can immediately identify with it. And cryptoscopophilia is also just a fun word, describing slightly risqué behavior that is certainly fun to talk about.

The reaction to cryptoscopophilia of a friend from Holland illustrates its positive prospects: he smiled and confidently told me that it was "the Dutch disease." After all, he explained, what else did they have to look at?

I doubt one could describe cryptoscopophilia as "the" or even "an" American disease because everyone is stuck in their cars, but not so the Dutch. They love cycling and walking and even have a word for "walking in the wind for fun"—*uitwaaien*.

So I am confident about cryptoscopophilia. In fact, I don't think it will be long before it earns its place in the OED where it will be flanked by a number of other interesting words formed with the crypto- prefix. Cryptoclimatology, for example, describes the hidden or secret microclimates of caves and other confined spaces. And cryptovolcanic structures (areas of underground volcanic activity) are apparently what scientists used to think caused the fragmented craters of what we now know are **astroblemes**.

❧ CRYPTOSCOPOPHILIA ALIVE

As Bill walked home from the Tube station (he was a passionate advocate for public transport) he discovered his natural **cryptoscopophilia** had been piqued a notch or two by his amorous mood. He couldn't wait to get home.

curglaff

{KUR-glahff. Noun.}

༄ MEANING

Curglaff also hasn't made it into the OED and, given it is more than 200 years old, it probably never will.

However, it did make it into the same helpful Scottish dictionary[28] that listed **bleezed**, so we know that it is Scottish dialect for "the shock felt in bathing, when one first plunges into the cold water."

The verb is **curgloff** and the adjective is **curgloft**.[29]

༄ AGE

Late 18th century

༄ ETYMOLOGY

Unfortunately, Jamieson's dictionary doesn't offer an etymology for curglaff, so I am left with the options of leaving this section blank or having a guess. I'll give it my best shot.

Cur is a Middle English word for "dog" that appears to be derived from the Old Norse onomatopoeic verb *kurra*, "to murmur, grumble." The OED goes on to suggest that "the primary sense appears thus to have been 'growling or snarling beast.'" If we add to that the (again, Scottish) noun gloff, "a sudden fright, scare, start" (OED), we end up with . . . a dog yelping as it splashes into a freezing cold Scottish stream.

༄ RARITY

Extremely rare

༄ WHY I LIKE THE WORD CURGLAFF

Like **bleezed** (and possibly **ballicatter**), curglaff is more evidence that the Scots simply have "a way" with words. And, because I cannot resist, here are three more delightful examples (all from Jamieson's dictionary): barlafumble, "An exclamation for a truce by one who has fallen down in wrestling or play"; ramfeezled: "Fatigued; exhausted"; and tentie: "Watchful; attentive. Cautious; careful. Intent; keen."

Curglaff

At first I try to gentle my way in
to pool or lake or ocean,
seeking to avoid suffering **curglaff**
but that's a hopeless notion;

the only way to get into the sea,
the pond or swimming hole,
is all at once, not inch by shivering inch—
curglaff's a thing to thole.†

† thole: archaic, still used in Scots dialect: endure, put up with

Elisabeth Danson, from *U.S. 1 Worksheets, Volume 44/45*
(Princeton University, 2002)

∾ CURGLAFF ALIVE

Bill arrived home to a house filled with Jane's arty designer friends. This, to him, was as effective an anaphrodisiac as the **curglaff** of a cold shower. But his disappointment was more than tempered by the sight of Jane actually having fun. And, sooner or later, the friends would have to leave.

cynosure

{SI-nə-shoor or SAI-noh-shoor. Noun.}

⬥ MEANING

According to the OED, cynosure has two distinct meanings:

1. The northern constellation Ursa Minor, which contains in its tail the Pole-star; also applied to the Pole-star itself.
2. *figuratively.* a. Something that serves for guidance or direction; a "guiding star." b. Something that attracts attention by its brilliancy or beauty; a center of attraction, interest, or admiration.

Neither the RH2 nor the W3 mentions the first meaning, but each, respectively, supplies a compelling citation to illustrate the second: "the cynosure of all eyes"; "the council too was a cynosure of the nation's hopes—*Time.*"

The adjective is **cynosural**.

⬥ AGE

Late 16th century

⬥ ETYMOLOGY

Cynosure is adopted from French and is an adaptation of the Latin *cynosura*, which was in turn adopted from Greek and which means, literally, "dog's tail." The connection to "Ursa Minor" is by way of our current northern pole star (Polaris), which is located in Ursa Minor's "tail." Ursa is the Latin for "bear" and Ursa Major means "great bear." Ursa Minor, therefore, means "little bear," and a little bear looks a bit like a dog, hence "dog's tail."

⬥ RARITY

Rare

⬥ WHY I LIKE THE WORD CYNOSURE

First, I love the etymology of cynosure. I have always been interested in astronomy but I know very little about it, so the connection to the pole star and Ursa Minor was immediately intriguing. And researching the word has pretty much doubled my knowledge of the subject. (I would need two postage stamps to write it to you now.)

I also love the concept of being drawn to something. A pole star needs to be visible and the position and brilliance of Polaris "attracts attention," just as the qualities of a cynosure become a focal point of admiration.

I think the word celebrity has lost its shine for most people, except perhaps the odd **arriviste**. So cynosure could offer us an opportunity to reward those truly deserving of admiration with a more appropriate and infinitely less tarnished label. I can certainly think of a few deserving candidates.

❦ CYNOSURE ALIVE

When Bill interviewed Ralph Addison, the unassuming 65-year-old now renting Rosamund's house next door, he had no idea the man was so popular. In fact, Bill had been a little concerned that Ralph might end up regularly needing their assistance, but nothing could be further from the truth. Ralph was a bona-fide **cynosure** and not a day passed without his receiving at least one visitor. All Bill knew about him was that he was from Bradford, that he was a widower and recently retired teacher, and that he wanted to experience life in London.

delitescent

{del-ə-TES-sənt. Adjective.}

❧ MEANING

As with **caliginous**, the definitions for delitescent are uncommonly concurrent (and brief).

OED: Lying hid, latent, concealed.

RH2: Concealed, hidden, latent.

W3: Lying hidden: obfuscated, latent.

The noun is **delitescence**.

❧ AGE

Late 17th century

❧ ETYMOLOGY

From the Latin *delitescere*, "to hide away."

❧ RARITY

Extremely rare

❧ WHY I LIKE THE WORD DELITESCENT

Three things attracted me to this word. The first was the uniformity of the definitions, which immediately piqued my interest. Next was the mysterious, almost scary nature of the word's meaning. Combining hidden with latent certainly fuels my imagination and, trust me, it hardly needs encouragement. Think sharks, crocodiles, snakes, plagues and all types of nasties. And the third (and biggest) hook was the OED's citation of the sentence by Sir William Hamilton quoted opposite.

I love the idea of "delitescent cognitions." Of course, all thoughts are "hidden," but Hamilton has powerfully summarized the premise of a major issue that I face every day in the writing and consulting work that I do. In an obsessively materialistic society, how do we raise the profile and perceived value of thought and consideration—activities that are essentially intangible?

How does this translate to our everyday lives? Here's an example. When I teach writing skills what I am really doing is asking people to think more and produce less. I am asking them to think about *why* they are writing—to whom, for what purpose? Then I am asking them to consider their words, critically, to establish if those words are likely to compel their readers to respond as they wish, or not. And, at the end of all this, they will invariably produce fewer words (a good thing for their readers). But, in materialistic terms, what they have done is spent more time and money producing less output. Concise messages may be successful where less-considered verbiage may fail, but their bosses don't have time to read these documents, they just want to see that the pages have been filled with words. Brevity is not the goal.

The sad reality of our frenzied and impatient economic culture is that not only are our cognitions delitescent, but so are their benefits. We don't have time to perceive value, or to recognize flaws and rip-offs. I wish I knew how to change this culture and its illogical standards but I don't. However, I do have some pretty good ideas about how to question it, and if I search for long enough I am bound to uncover a few solutions.

Let us take a moment to consider the value of the word delitescent. Do we really need it? Maybe, maybe not, but I challenge you to substitute it from Hamilton's sentence without losing something that was worth keeping.

❧ DELITESCENT ALIVE

Ralph Addison had been revealed by one of his many visitors to be a modest and dedicated professional whose unceasing promotion of the typically **delitescent** talents of his students had resulted in his positively affecting the lives of thousands of them. Most of these students were now adults living successful lives and, clearly, a fair few of them lived in London. Probably despite his efforts to not be a burden on anyone, word had got out about his move to London. Bill and Jane were proud to be his neighbors.

desipience

{də-SIP-ee-əns. Noun; also **desipiency**.}

༄ MEANING

The OED's definition of desipience, "folly; foolish trifling, silliness," attracted my attention; the W3's definition, "relaxed dallying in enjoyment of foolish trifles," fixed it.

The adjective is **desipient**.

༄ AGE

Mid-17th century

༄ ETYMOLOGY

From the Latin *desipientia*, formed from *desipere*, "to be foolish."

༄ RARITY

Extremely rare

༄ WHY I LIKE THE WORD DESIPIENCE

I adore this word and I nearly had to handcuff myself to not use its adjective when I was discussing those flea-picking monkeys back in the **antinomy** entry. Desipient monkeys. Yes, that feels better.

So, "foolish trifling, silliness" and (my favorite) "relaxed dallying." Are these important things for which we need a special group adjective? Bally right, we do.

I am absolutely convinced that a significant component of our frenzied, over-consumptive way of life is our flawed assumption that we *should be* important, busy people. As soon as city folk escape to the wilderness they relax; this is because the physical and temporal scale of really big things, like mountain ranges, recalibrates humans. Subconsciously, it reminds us that we are here for a very short time, *unlike* mountain ranges. In a thousand years from now a mountain range will still be a mountain range dominating the skyline and leaving city folk helpfully awestruck, whereas we will be precisely nothing, and will have been so for most of that time.

Put another way, we don't, in the grand scheme of things, have a whole lot

riding on what we do with our individual lives—passing that exam or getting
that promotion are as important as we choose to make them: they are not
inherently important. So it is okay to play and have fun and be silly. If you are
a child, desipience is your job. And if you are an adult, desipience is part of
your job. Our senses of humor and ability to laugh would not have evolved
if they were not essential. So, just as we need to rate more highly serious
consideration, we need to do the same for desipience.

Now, it seems a bit pompous to be dedicating words but, well, too bad.
I lovingly dedicate this word to my daughter, Gabriella, a master of "foolish
trifling." She is a fairy in a little girl's body and she reminds me every day how
much I enjoy laughter and silliness.

ꙮ DESIPIENCE ALIVE

Bill knew that what Jane and Rosamund enjoyed doing most together was
laughing and having fun, and he knew his wife would be in need of some
concerted **desipience**. He took her to see *The Complete Works of William
Shakespeare* by the reduced, Reduced Shakespeare Company; one of the three
multi-part playing actors was sick, and the remaining two were quite manic
and absolutely brilliant.

divagate

{DAI-və-geyt. Verb.}

MEANING

Divagate (note the "di" rhymes with high) has one clear meaning with two distinct contexts.

To divagate is to "wander about" or "stray," either in the physical sense or in discourse. So you can divagate from one place to another, or from one subject to another.

As you may have just been thinking, divagate is certainly a synonym of digress, but they don't appear to be entirely synonymous (which is a good thing because, if this were so, one of them would have to "go"—you know; the chop, gone, *obsolete*). Usage suggests that a person who strays just once from a topic is digressing, but a person who strays more than once or who strays in more than one direction is divagating.

AGE

Late 16th century

ETYMOLOGY

From the Latin *divagatus*, past participle of *divagari*, "to wander off," which is formed from the prefix *di-*, "apart," and the verb *vagari*, "to wander."

RARITY

Very rare

WHY I LIKE THE WORD DIVAGATE

I have non-identical twin daughters with dichotomous, but complementary, personalities. So Pascale, totally unlike Gabriella, is Busy Scientist Girl. Unfortunately for her, Pascale appears to have inherited my restless mind and ridiculously broad interests so, just like me, she divagates (digressing is for wimps). Of course, this actually makes me feel quite useful (being able to empathize with her and help her with things) and, accordingly, I lovingly dedicate this word to her.

Divagate is a particularly interesting word, not so much because of its meaning, but because of its popularity (or should I say, its unpopularity).

Just a guess, but I reckon you probably use the word navigate more often than you use the word divagate. Okay, it wasn't a guess because, according to Google.com, navigate appears on about 6000 *times* more web pages than divagate. That data suggests divagate is 1/6000th as popular a word and yet, in our household, a full half of our family (that's Pascale and me) divagate as much as we navigate. (Pascale, bless her, is not "fixed" on anything. She doesn't have favorites, she has favorites *this* week. *Next* week is a whole new deal.)

What this tells us is that we are an innately hopeful lot who often choose words that describe the behaviors we aspire to, rather than the ones we actually display. The truth is that every time we navigate towards something or someone we are, in some way, divagating away from something or someone else (otherwise we would all have bursting wardrobes and far too many friends). For every new fashion, something has to fall out of fashion.

❧ DIVAGATE ALIVE

Jane had started to get used to her day-to-day life without having Rosamund next door. But some days she found herself knocked completely off course by her little sister's absence. On those days she **divagated** from her tasks at work, wandering off here and there to muse about memories of Jane-and-Rosamund-activities; the things she didn't do any more.

dolorifuge

{də-LOR-(r)ə-fyooj. Noun.}

MEANING

The W3 defines dolorifuge as "something that banishes or mitigates grief."

The adjective is **dolorifugic**.

AGE

Late 19th century

ETYMOLOGY

Formed from dolor, "sorrow, grief" (from the Middle English *dolour*, from the Latin *dolor*, from *dolere*, "to feel pain, grieve"), and the combining form -fuge, "one that drives away," from the Latin *fugare*, "to put to flight."

RARITY

Extremely rare

WHY I LIKE THE WORD DOLORIFUGE

This is a beautiful and engaging word. I know from experience that time is the only thing you can rely on to drive away grief, but I am inspired by the hopefulness of dolorifuge—that something other than time might reduce that pain and distress.

The word's etymology gives me a clue as to how dolorifuge might occur. For something to "take flight" it needs to be untethered. So dolorifuge is the trigger that breaks the hold that grief has over you. I guess that trigger could be anything, but it is most likely to be the introduction of something new, something to fill at least some portion of the gap left by your loss. And therein lies the hope: new experiences, new connections, new interests, new goals.

When we grieve we expect sympathy, we hope for empathy but, eventually, we need dolorifuge.

⤫ QUOTATION ⤫

Meanwhile Tess was walking thoughtfully among the gooseberry-bushes in the garden, and over Prince's grave.

When she came in her mother pursued her advantage.

"Well, what be you going to do?" she asked.

. . . "I don't know what to say!" answered the girl restlessly. "It is for you to decide. I killed the old horse, and I suppose I ought to do something to get ye a new one. But - but - I don't quite like Mr d'Urberville being there!"

The children, who had made use of this idea of Tess being taken up by their wealthy kinsfolk (which they imagined the other family to be) as a species of **dolorifuge** after the death of the horse, began to cry at Tess's reluctance, and teased and reproached her for hesitating.

"Tess won't go - o - o and be made a la - a - dy of! - no, she says she wo - o—on't!" they wailed, with square mouths. "And we shan't have a nice new horse, and lots o' golden money to buy fairlings! And Tess won't look pretty in her best cloze no mo - o - ore!"

Thomas Hardy, *Tess of the D'Urbervilles* (1891)[31]

⤫ DOLORIFUGE ALIVE

Tomorrow would be Rosamund's birthday. Bill was not a birthday person, but Jane and Rosamund were and they always made a big deal of the day for each other. Bill knew that Jane was suffering from a kind of grief and that he needed to find a **dolorifuge**. He hoped the ticket to Chicago he had just given Jane would do the trick and took the flow of "happy tears" streaming down her face as a positive sign.

drachenfutter

{DRAH-khən-foot-ə. Noun.}

❧ MEANING

According to Howard Rheingold, author of *They Have a Word for It: A Lighthearted Lexicon of Untranslatable Words & Phrases* (Severn House, 1988), *Drachenfutter* (with or without an initial capital) is "a peace offering from guilty husbands for wives."

❧ AGE

Late 20th century

❧ ETYMOLOGY

In etymological parlance, this word is OOO (of obscure origin). This is just slightly flakier than being OUO (of unknown origin). Other than *Drachenfutter* clearly being a loanword from German, I don't know who, if anyone, used it in English before Rheingold (and he was only "translating" it), and I don't know anything about its coinage or usage in German. I can't find it in *any* dictionary, English or German.

What I do know (or, at least, can confidently guess) is that *Drachenfutter* is formed from the German prefix *Drachen-*, which can mean either "dragon" or "kite" (not the bird), and *Futter*, "feed, fodder, animal food." Presumably, then, *futter* refers to Rheingold's "peace offering" and *Drachen* refers to the recipient of that conciliatory gift. That only leaves us to work out whether "wife" is synonymous with dragon or kite. My guess (just a shot in the dark) is dragon.

Drachenfutter is listed in Christopher J. Moore's recent book, *In Other Words* (Walker & Company, 2004), but other than that book and Rheingold's book, I can't find any other published instances of the word.

The Internet Movie Database (IMDB.com) lists *Drachenfutter* as the title of a 1987 West German film directed by Jan Schütte. It provides two English translations, *Dragon Chow* and *Dragon's Food*. I don't know if the film has anything to do with guilty husbands and fire-breathing dragons.

❧ RARITY

Extremely rare

❧ QUOTATION ❧

I went out drinking with my friends again last night, so I had to bring back some **drachenfutter** for Gretchen, my new girlfriend.

Jonathan Keith Sheriff, Merriam-Webster
OnLine Open Dictionary (web forum), 26 Oct. 2005[32]

❧ WHY I LIKE THE WORD DRACHENFUTTER

Okay, I'll admit it. This word is so O-for-obscure that I probably shouldn't have chosen it. But I did, because I want it to survive. I want to be able to blab about it (in a silly German accent) with my friends at the bar, boasting about how much *Drachenfutter* I had to cough up for my latest screw-up.

Drachenfutter really is a word custom-built for men. It's not that we like the idea of getting caught and having to pay up, but I think the idea of being forgiven—especially by "the dragon"—is hugely appealing. According to Rheingold, at one obscure point in time, it was common to see German men on a Saturday afternoon already in possession of the *Drachenfutter* they knew they were going to need much later that night.

And remember all those synonyms for **bleezed**? Well, it is obvious to me that all those words and phrases exist because drunk people become very creative, and drunk people like to talk about just how drunk they are. They also like to talk about, well, their "dragons." And so I wonder if the concept that has the next highest number of synonyms (after inebriated) might be dragon, cow, battle-axe, hag, tart, bag, etc., etc.

❧ DRACHENFUTTER ALIVE

Jane arrived in Chicago in time for a birthday breakfast with Rosamund. Angelo had apparently been so excited about Jane's arrival that he had forgotten to come home the night before and arrived at the airport (just moments before Jane exited Customs), laden with some of the most expensive ***Drachenfutter*** Jane had ever seen (including, Jane noted, some very tasty looking chocolates).

elozable

{ə-LO-zah-bəl. Adjective.}

ᴧ MEANING
The OED defines elozable as "amenable to flattery."

ᴧ AGE
Mid-16th century

ᴧ ETYMOLOGY
The OED suggests (it says "as if") the word is derived from the Old French *eslosable*, formed from *esloser*, "to praise." I have no other suggestions and I cannot find the word in any other dictionaries so the OED's suggestion will have to do.

ᴧ RARITY
Extremely rare

ᴧ WHY I LIKE THE WORD ELOZABLE
When designating the rarity of the words in this book I have used three grades: rare, very rare, and extremely rare. For a word like elozable, I really need a fourth option: extinct. This word is way past obsolete, it is dead and buried. So can we, should we, attempt to breathe life back into it?

I'll answer that question with three more: Do you know anyone who *isn't* amenable to flattery? Is it more concise to say "elozable" or "amenable to flattery"? Is there any reason why we shouldn't attempt to breathe life back into a word that uniquely describes such a universal human quality?

Whatever your answers, I know I am going to use this word, particularly in the context of my gorgeous wife who is gloriously elozable. And I am also going to lovingly dedicate this word to her (and now that's all three of my gals duly acknowledged; important box checked).

One of the qualities I particularly like about elozable (in addition to its remarkable rarity) is its polite understatement. And this reminds me of an even rarer ("deader!") word: avidulous.

Avidulous means "somewhat greedy" (OED). That's it. The polite understatement reminded me of the late Douglas Adams, the master of this important art form who used *The Hitchhiker's Guide to the Galaxy* to describe earth as "mostly harmless."

So should we also breathe life into avidulous? Absolutely, and I have empirical data to back up my call. The phrase "somewhat greedy" is common vernacular—Google.com lists more than 3,000 web pages that include the phrase—so it needs its own word. And, given how greedy we are and how many different ways we can be greedy, I am sure we need more words that mean "greedy" (think Eskimo and snow; Arabs and camel).

⟨ ELOZABLE ALIVE

Despite her plans to despise him, Jane was surprised to find herself enjoying Angelo's considerable charms, as she had when she worked for him. Like most Italian men, Angelo appreciated the fact that all women were **elozable** and he had worked hard over the years to find new and original ways to flatter them. Added to his effort was a knack for making a woman feel important. He certainly made Rosamund feel that way.

fortuity

{for-TCHOO-ə-tee. Noun; also **fortuitousness**.}

MEANING

For this word I specifically want to compare the OED and RH2 definitions head-to-head.

OED: "Fortuitous character, fortuitousness; accident, chance; an accidental occurrence. Occasionally used for: Appearance of fortuitousness or unstudiedness." RH2: "1. the state or quality of being fortuitous; fortuitous character. 2. an accidental occurrence. 3. an instance of great luck or good fortune."

The adjective is **fortuitous** and the adverb is **fortuitously**.

AGE

Mid-18th century

ETYMOLOGY

From the Latin *fortuitus*, formed from *forte*, "by chance," formed from *fors*, "chance," and -ity.

RARITY

Very rare

WHY I LIKE THE WORD FORTUITY

The incongruent definitions of the OED and RH2 interest me. Is the change it belies a good thing, a bad thing, or an adiaphoron ("an indifferent thing," remember the stoic concept, adiaphora, from **ataraxia**)?

And here's another question—When people ask you if something is good or bad, do they usually also add "or indifferent"? Do you see where I am going with this?

Not everything is good or bad, some things just don't matter. And not everything that happens is good luck or bad luck, some things just happen. But something in our make-up fights this truth and makes chance and indifference unpalatable to us. Wherever chance and indifference lurk, we ignore them, expel them, or mislabel them. And I guess we think this makes our lives more important and more meaningful. But in altering the truth we lose something important; in this case we lose a set of words that were specifically set aside to denote randomness and, in doing so, we push that universal truth even further away.

So I am not suggesting we turn back time and expunge the lucky connotation from fortuity, fortuitous, and fortuitously; I am simply posting a warning in the hope that I will encourage you to resist change in similar circumstances. That said, I do hold out some small hope that fortuity's rarity might just mean its original meaning *can* be saved.

And I know I will already have the support of the legal community who use both fortuity ("mere fortuity") and fortuitous ("a fortuitous event") specifically for their original meanings, as illustrated in the quotation.[35]

⟨ FORTUITY ALIVE

When Jane returned to London, she found her guilt about having introduced Rosamund and Angelo to each other waiting patiently for her. Bill knew he needed to quickly break the spell.

"Let it go, darling. It doesn't mean anything. Angelo was merely a client. Rosie met him as she has most of your clients. And they happened to click. That's all there is to it. It's just **fortuity**. It's not you."

foudroyant

{foo-DROI-ənt or (French) foo-DRWAH-yahng. Adjective.}

ᴓ MEANING

The dictionaries agree that foudroyant has two definitions, a general one and a medical (or, specifically, pathological) one. They are also in agreement about those definitions, but I will opt for the RH2's entry: "1. striking as with lightning; sudden and overwhelming in effect; stunning; dazzling. 2. *Pathol.* (of disease) beginning in a sudden and severe form." The OED and W3 both mention "thundering."

Combine them, as Wiktionary has done, and you get: "Having an awesome and overwhelming effect."

The noun is **foudroyance** and the adverb is **foudroyantly**.

ᴓ AGE

Mid-19th century

ᴓ ETYMOLOGY

Foudroyant is a loanword from French, formed from *foudroyer*, "to strike with or as with lightning," which was derived from *foudre*, "lightning; a thunderbolt."

ᴓ RARITY

Very rare

ᴓ WHY I LIKE THE WORD FOUDROYANT

The *Harrap's Shorter French Dictionary* (1996) on my bookshelf translates *foudroyant* as simply "devastating." When you think about the meanings above, this really is what this word means. And its pertinence to disease only enhances the poignancy of this quality. Certainly, none of us wants to be struck down with a foudroyant form of any disease.

The "striking power" of foudroyant was the primary reason I selected the word for my list, but I confess there is another, less important but possibly more interesting, reason why I like this word: the ambiguity of its two standard (but distinct) pronunciations.

Which will (or do) you use, the Anglicized one or the French one? And why? A choice like this can be significant because it can be a barrier to ever using the word in speech. *What if I choose the French pronunciation and they think I'm being snooty; or I choose the English pronunciation and they think I'm being base?* **Arriviste** presents a similar issue but, given there is an acknowledged anglicized variant spelling, **arrivist**, the choice seems less personal. Words are seldom just words: letters combining to communicate a single standard meaning. Our very choice of words, pronunciation, accent and grammar all reveal more to our audiences than we sometimes wish.

⦿ FOUDROYANT ALIVE

Something clicked in Jane: She was released. The change was **foudroyant**, affecting every part of her life. The confident and vivacious Jane was back and she was ready to do some catching up. It had been two months since she last went on a serious shopping spree, so that would be the ideal activity with which to launch her renaissance. Of course, she would need help and Rosamund wasn't available, so Bill would have to do.

glandaceous

{glan-DEY-shəs. Adjective.}

❧ MEANING
From the OED: "Acorn colored."

This is obviously one of the shorter definitions in the OED and, usually, I am a big fan of brevity, but in this case I think the definition is too brief. For clarity, I propose expanding the definition to "the yellowish-brown color of a ripe acorn."

❧ AGE
Late 19th century

❧ ETYMOLOGY
From the Latin *glans, glandis,* "acorn" (possibly via the French, *gland*), and the suffix -aceous, "of the nature of."

❧ RARITY
Extremely rare

❧ WHY I LIKE THE WORD GLANDACEOUS
Spend an hour with an interior designer and you will quickly learn there is so much more to describing color than qualifying primary and secondary colors as being either "light" or "dark." The reality is that if you earnestly investigate any color you will uncover an entire palate of subtle and not-so-subtle variations.

For example, let us consider my favorite color, blue. At the pale end we have Alice blue, baby blue, powder blue, periwinkle, turquoise, and aquamarine. In the middle hues we have Columbia blue, cornflower blue, dodger blue, azure, steel blue, cerulean, and denim. And at the dark end of the blue spectrum there is Persian blue, cobalt blue, ultramarine, royal blue, navy blue, sapphire, Prussian blue, and midnight blue. Consider further that this list is far from exhaustive and it may seem to you, as it does to me, that more of us are color-blind than we think!

❧ GLANDACEOUS ALIVE

Jane wanted to get a head start on the day and had dragged Bill along with her to where they now stood at the door to her favorite boutique, waiting for it to open. When it did, they had the shop to themselves, which really rather suited Bill—he hated crowds. And Jane was in her element, bringing the colors to life for Bill.

"That's burgundy, Bill. This is carmine. That's amaranth. And that you could probably call sangria. Do you see the differences? It's never red, Bill, never red. What about this skirt—what color do you think it is?'

Now Bill was on the spot. "Mustard?" he offered, as tentatively as he could.

"Good try, Bill, good try. I'd say **glandaceous**."

handsel

{HAN(D)-səl. Noun and verb; also **hansel**.}

∾ MEANING

As a noun, a handsel is (according to the RH2):

1. A gift or token for good luck or as an expression of good wishes, as at the beginning of the new year or when entering upon a new situation or enterprise.
2. A first installment of payment.
3. The initial experience of anything; first encounter with or use of something taken as a token of what will follow; foretaste.

And as a verb, to handsel is (again, from the RH2): "to give a handsel to; to inaugurate auspiciously; to use, try, or experience for the first time."

The OED adds that handsel is also used in Handsel Monday: "the first Monday of the year" when, in Scotland, "New Year's handsel is given." Apparently this used to be a big deal (even more important than Hogmanay) because not only did workers receive handsel (usually a cash gift), but other than the odd day off to attend the local fair, Handsel Monday was their only holiday for the entire year.

The OED also mentions that handsel can be a "luck-penny," which was once literally a penny but later became any sum of money that a buyer gives to a seller (usually of livestock) to bring good fortune to the deal. I understand this money is quickly used up to buy the first round of drinks at the pub, which is how I think we should all celebrate deals.

∾ AGE

Early 13th century

∾ ETYMOLOGY

Oh yes, indeed, this is a *very* old word: both the OED and the RH2 estimate the date of origin as 1050 (the 13th-century date above refers to the first written citation). The word appeared variously as *handselne, hansell,* or *handsellen* (as a verb) in Middle English, with the sense of "good luck token," and was probably derived from the Old Norse *handsal* or *handseld*, "an obligation confirmed with a handshake" or from the Old English *handselen*, "giving into the hands of another" (OED).

∽ RARITY
Very rare

∽ WHY I LIKE THE WORD HANDSEL
Back when Christmas didn't mean receiving 12 weeks' worth of junk mail, and there was time to get into the spirit of the festival rather than the spirit of commerce, I really enjoyed the gift-giving aspect of it. But for many years that enjoyment waned as the whole thing became an obligation to be endured rather than an activity to be savored. Today, my family has successfully reclaimed Christmas, but the idea of a handsel, a gift given to partners (domestic or commercial) at the beginning of January to bring luck to the new year's endeavors, really appeals.

∽ HANDSEL ALIVE
After the third time Bill said "So, I guess we'd better be getting home now," Jane made very sure that Bill understood that such musings were not part of shopping etiquette and were best kept to himself. Bill was contrite: "I'm sorry, darling. I won't say another word. I don't know the drill. Remember, this is a **handsel** for me. But I'll learn."

holophrasis

{hə-loh-FRAY-səss or hə-LOF-frah-sis. Noun.}

༄ MEANING

A holophrasis, however you choose to pronounce it, is "the expression of a whole phrase or combination of ideas by one word" (OED). I really like that.

Have you still performed a holophrasis if you only manage to get your "combination of ideas" down to two or three words? No, according to the definitions of all three dictionaries, but yes if you go by one of the OED's citations: "the reduction of whole sentences into words."[37]

The product of holophrasis is a holophrase: "*Philology.* A single word used instead of a phrase, or to express a combination of ideas (e.g. ungetatable)" (OED).

༄ AGE
Late 19th century

༄ ETYMOLOGY
From the Greek *holo-*, "whole," and *phrases*, "speech."

༄ RARITY
Extremely rare

༄ WHY I LIKE THE WORD HOLOPHRASIS

Capturing a whole phrase or idea in a single word is seldom easy, at least for adults, but toddlers perform holophrasis with almost everything they say. We cannot get away with demanding "ball" when we want someone to pass us a ball, but it is precisely what you expect a toddler to say and is a bona fide example of holophrasis in action.

I expect every society has a few beloved holophrases that not only communicate "a whole phrase in a word," but also provide information about the psyche of the speakers. For example, here in New Zealand our national holophrase is (without a doubt) "bugger."

It would be fair to say, given the word's original meaning of "a sodomite," that this is a peculiar choice for what is effectively a national icon, but that's just the way it is. What does it mean to them? Well, it means a few things, which is why it is such a wonderful holophrase. It means (and I will try to be precise) "damn it, that didn't work out as I had planned and that probably means I'm screwed because I've missed the boat and you can't unbreak an egg and, just to make things that little bit worse, I really should have seen that coming and not got myself into this mess in the first place." Yep, that about says it all.

    Languages that compound their words (like German) are naturally at an advantage when it comes to creating a holophrase, but as with any process of combining things there is an art to it, and the Germans are masters of this art. Consider this beauty: *Torschlüsspanik*, "a sense of alarm or anxiety (said to be experienced particularly in middle age) caused by the feeling that life's opportunities are passing (or have passed) one by; spec. that manifested in an ageing woman who longs to rediscover the (sexual) excitement of youth, and who fears being left 'on the shelf'" (OED). The literal translation of *Torschlüsspanik* is "panic at the shutting of the door."

❧ HOLOPHRASIS ALIVE

Bill saw her put down the phone; the blood had drained from her face. "Accident?" he asked, instantly worried.

    Jane shook her head.

    "Pregnant?'

    Jane shook her head again. She needed only one word, but the result of her **holophrasis** was a word that Bill would not soon forget: "Engaged."

imbroglio

{eem-BROL-yoh. Noun; also **embroglio**.}

ᴗ MEANING

There are always at least two sides to an imbroglio, but the OED appears to have capably captured them all:

1. A confused heap.
2. A state of great confusion and entanglement; a complicated or difficult situation (*esp.* political or dramatic); a confused misunderstanding or disagreement, embroilment.
3. "A passage, in which the vocal or instrumental parts are made to sing, or play, against each other, in such a manner as to produce the effect of apparent but really well-ordered confusion." (Grove *Dict. Mus.* 1880)

ᴗ AGE

Mid-18th century

ᴗ ETYMOLOGY

Imbroglio is a loanword from Italian, formed from *imbrogliare*, "to embroil, entangle," and is cognate with (and probably derived from) the Middle French verb *embrouiller*, "to muddle, embroil."

ᴗ RARITY

Rare

ᴗ WHY I LIKE THE WORD IMBROGLIO

Imbroglios (apparently, *imbrogli* is not used in English[39]) are an unavoidable part of life, so it is great to have a word that both defines these awkward situations and captures their spirit. An imbroglio is not a mess, a pickle, or a complicated situation—they are all condiments to the imbroglio's staple: confusion. And confusion is often funny and always "human." This is why we love to follow imbroglios on the big screen, the small screen and the stage.

Let's look at the components of an imbroglio based on that model of verismo (OED: "realism or naturalism in the arts"), the film *Notting Hill*, in

❧ QUOTATION ❧

At the same time a great and troubled curiosity,
and a certain chill of fear, possessed his spirit. The conduct of
the man with the chin-beard, the terms of the letter, and the
explosion of the early morning, fitted together like parts in some
obscure and mischievous **imbroglio**. Evil was certainly afoot . . .

Robert Louis Stevenson and Fanny Van De Grift Stevenson,
More New Arabian Nights: The Dynamiter
(Longmans, Green & Co., 1885)

which we have Hugh Grant, playing the English bookshop owner, falling
for Julia Roberts, the American film star. There are forgotten phone messages,
Julia's ex, the vile British tabloids and countless misunderstandings all
conspiring to keep Julia out of Hugh's loving arms. The protagonists are both
involved in the confusion (an important component); it's not a side issue. And
there are layers—there always have to be layers. Metaphorically, I think of an
imbroglio as a ball of tangled spaghetti: messy, complicated and difficult (but
fun) to untangle.

❧ IMBROGLIO ALIVE

The **imbroglio** that followed was predictable but unhelpful because it didn't
actually involve the main protagonist, Rosamund. Jane and Rosamund's
parents had both died when the girls were teenagers, but there were plenty of
others with whom Jane could dissect and redissect the news. Eventually, Bill
had to step in and tell her straight: "Call her. Talk to her."

inamorata

{een-ahm-oh-RAH-tə. Noun; also **enamorata**.}

MEANING

From the OED: "A female lover, mistress, sweetheart."

A lover, mistress, *or* sweetheart—there's latitude for you. The W3 leans mistress-ward with "a woman with whom one is in love or has intimate relations; specifically mistress." The RH2 leans in a different direction with "a woman who loves or is loved; female sweetheart or lover."

The masculine equivalent of inamorata, as you might have already guessed, is **inamorato**.

AGE

Mid-17th century

ETYMOLOGY

Inamorata is a loanword from Italian, formed from *innamorare*, which means "to inflame (or inspire) with love." *Brava!*

RARITY

Rare

WHY I LIKE THE WORD INAMORATA

Stumbling across this word was pure serendipity.

Like anyone in a long-term relationship, I have to make countless decisions about how to address and refer to my partner (in my case, my wife, Simone). Besides her name and its diminutive (Sim), what have my options been? The traditional choice of endearments seems to be Dear, Darling, Love, Sweetheart, Honey and, once a year, the hackneyed Valentine. But does any one of those terms befit a gorgeous, made-up woman in a perfectly selected evening dress? I think not, but Gorgeous itself works so I have employed it (many times).

Today's world of cappuccinos and lattes has thrown up the effervescent bella (Italian for "beautiful"), which I find exudes joyfulness at every utterance. But radiant-looking daughters and female friends can all be bellas, and that

still left me short of a word with which to describe the woman with whom I
am totally enamored—and embroiled!

❧ INAMORATA ALIVE

Jane put down the phone and returned to the kitchen where Bill was leaning
over the sink, still in shock. He turned to Jane, "It just doesn't sound like Rosie
to move this fast," he said, hoping Jane would now tell him it was all a silly
joke—or one of Angelo's tall stories.

Jane looked resigned. "He called her his **inamorata**, Bill. He gave her a
diamond necklace. What could I say to that? Oh no, he's just making it all up
and you should turn him down because your silly sister thinks she saw him kiss
her assistant months ago."

"You *did* see him."

"Maybe, but it doesn't change anything. It's too late."

incompossible

{in-kom-POS-sə-bəl. Adjective.}

ᐧᐁ MEANING

The W3 defines incompossible as "not mutually possible: inconsistent, incompatible." The OED takes it up a notch with "not possible together; wholly incompatible or inconsistent; hence, **incompossibility**."

ᐧᐁ AGE

Early 17th century

ᐧᐁ ETYMOLOGY

From the Latin, *incompossibilis*, "not jointly possible," formed from the Latin *in-*, "not," and the mediaeval Latin *compossibilis*, which is in turn formed from *com-*, "jointly" and *possibilis*, "possible."

ᐧᐁ RARITY

Extremely rare

ᐧᐁ WHY I LIKE THE WORD INCOMPOSSIBLE

This is one of those words that makes you think. What does "not mutually possible" actually mean? What is *wholly* incompatible? And how does incompossibility relate to mutual exclusivity and incompatibility?

Distinguishing between incompossible and incompatible is, for me, the easiest part of this analysis (despite the W3 unhelpfully including incompatible, without qualification, in its definition). People who don't "work well" together are incompatible, but people who *cannot* be together, for whatever reason, are incompossible. So you might have incompatible friends who, for everyone's benefit, you prefer to keep separate. But you *could* put these two people in the same room—it might be unwise, but it is possible. In terms of incompossibility, your friends themselves cannot be incompossible, they *can* both exist, but their being in the same room tomorrow can be incompossible if, for example, one of them is halfway up Mt. Everest and the other one is with you, in New York. Sure, the US military might potentially be able to airlift both of them to a rendezvous in Turkey, but the chances of you convincing them to do it in time are nil.

And what of mutual exclusivity? Mutual exclusivity is actually a logical concept distinguishing the causality of events. For example, most events are independent. *I parked my car this morning. I sat on my glasses this afternoon.* But some events are mutually exclusive. *I parked my car this morning. I drove my car all morning without stopping.*

So, to summarize, incompatible elements don't work well together, mutually exclusive events are not simultaneously possible because of each event's qualities, and incompossible elements or events cannot occur simultaneously because of the laws of the universe. Clear as mud?

⌘ INCOMPOSSIBLE ALIVE

As the wedding plans took shape, Jane knew there were going to have to be compromises. At the top of Rosamund's wish list was people—family and friends—and lots of them. And just below that (just above "gorgeous wedding dress") was one tiny but significant word: Fiji. Focusing on the wedding dress would clearly need to be the strategy because the other two wishes were **incompossible**.

infonesia

{in-foh-NEE-zjə. Noun.}

∾ MEANING

Infonesia is a neologism that hasn't yet made it into any of the three dictionaries, but is defined by MSN Encarta as: "Inability to remember location of information: inability to remember an item of information or its location, especially on the Internet (informal)."

The TechEncyclopedia from TechWeb.com has a more extensive definition.

> **infonesia**: (INFOrmation amNESIA) Forgetting the source of some information. The single biggest problem of the information age is "too much information" from mail, e-mail, newspapers, magazines, radio, TV and the Web. Internesia (INTERnet amNESIA) is the Internet-only version of infonesia, when you forget the address of the Web site that had something of interest to you.

∾ AGE

Late 20th century

∾ ETYMOLOGY

As explained above, infonesia is a neologism formed by combining info- from information and -nesia from amnesia. I cannot find a reference to the coiner of this word, but it follows a common pattern of combining info- as a prefix with a range of other words. Two of my favorites are infoglut ("an excess of information") and infobahn ("the information superhighway").

∾ RARITY

Very rare

∾ WHY I LIKE THE WORD INFONESIA

Like anyone speeding without restriction on the infobahn, I regularly suffer from infonesia, so it is handy to have a term that rightfully shifts at least some of the blame from my failing memory to the ridiculously excessive quantity of information that I, like you, have to negotiate on a daily basis.

And infonesia will only get worse—*if* we let it. I totally agree with the observation that "the single biggest problem of the information age is "too much information."" The positive benefits of having universal access to the vast majority of the world's data, information and knowledge are significant, but the reality is that access is far from universal and, in any case, quantity has totally overwhelmed quality, leaving it easy to find numerous instances of the same fact or figure, but difficult to gain useful knowledge.

If my wife and I do nothing to protect our girls from the 24-hour madness of life on the infobahn, they will have to negotiate for themselves an all-consuming suite of electrical devices that invariably result in users exercising, relaxing and sleeping less. So we have made choices and we will continue to make choices to help them negotiate threats to their health and well-being that we did not have to deal with. I estimate that, in first-world countries, most 10-year-olds have already been exposed to more information than their grandparents had access to in their entire lives. But information is not knowledge, experience, understanding, empathy or appreciation. As the new generations fend off terabytes of information, will they ever find the time and mental space to learn and truly comprehend the principles of science, nature and human life?

INFONESIA ALIVE

Bill was sure he had seen a fantastic special for Fiji holidays on the web, but a regular bout of **infonesia** meant he couldn't remember where.

"Use your History, Darling," Jane reminded him.

"My what?'

"Your History tool. In the browser."

Bill looked at Jane blankly.

"Never mind, Bill, it really doesn't matter."

irenical

{ai-REN-ə-kəl or ai-REEN-ə-kəl. Adjective; also **eirenical**, **irenic**.}

ᴄᴅ MEANING

The W3 defines irenical as "conducive to or operating toward peace, moderation, harmony, and conciliation and away from contention and partisanship especially among disputants."

The OED and RH2 both define irenical as "tending to promote peace," though the OED qualifies the statement with "esp. in relation to theological or ecclesiastical differences."

The W3 lists "pacific" as a synonym; the OED includes it as part of its definition. The OED and RH2 also both include "peaceful" as part of their definitions, with the RH2 adding "conciliatory."

The adverb is **irenically**, "in the spirit of peace" (OED).

ᴄᴅ AGE

Mid-17th century

ᴄᴅ ETYMOLOGY

From the Greek *eirïnikos*, formed from *eirïnï*, "peace," and *-ikos*, -ic.

ᴄᴅ RARITY

Extremely rare

ᴄᴅ WHY I LIKE IRENICAL

The way the world is right now—armed *and* crowded—it seems to me this is a word that we all need to know about.

To conduct yourself in an irenical manner is not merely to be conciliatory, or to arbitrarily diffuse tensions or douse tempers, it is to "promote peace" and that means actively searching out that which connects us over that which separates us.

This word inspires me, just as its antonym—polemic—frightens me. Conflict will always be attractive to the few who crave power and control, and if there is less energy devoted to irenical activities than to polemic activities, then the polemics will prosper and the rest of us will suffer. Wars over religion and (more scarily, to me at least) resources loom before us and I believe we need to be working much harder now to head off these threats before they overwhelm us. It is always easier to change attitudes and habits than it is to wage wars, and yet we so often take for granted what we have and invest far too little in education, conservation and conciliation.

Before moving on, a quick note about the quotation. It is from an extensive and colorful online biography of dubious authority. Hyperbole is *de rigueur* and the entire thing appears to be based on *Appleton's Cyclopedia*, which was notorious for including around 200 fictitious entries. I suppose this could be one of them.

⚬ IRENICAL ALIVE

Rosamund chose an expensive resort in Fiji for her wedding venue and then concluded that the reason more than half of her friends indicated they wouldn't be able to attend was because "they all hate Angelo and they all hate me." It didn't matter how many times Jane assured her that affordability was the true cause of the responses, Rosamund simply refused to listen to reason. Jane eventually had to ask Bill to step in and play the **irenical** brother-in-law and, unexpectedly, it worked. But even more unexpectedly, Rosamund then announced that, despite her and Jane knowing a dozen dressmakers, she had chosen "a friend" of Angelo's to make her "gorgeous wedding dress." For Jane, this was proof that Rosamund was completely out of her mind.

juste milieu

{ZHUST-mee-lyer. Noun.}

MEANING

The OED defines a juste milieu as "the happy medium, the golden mean; judicious moderation, esp. in politics," and illustrates this with a short citation from a 1945 book on German history:[43] "One looks in vain in their history for a *juste milieu*, for common sense."

This citation appears somewhat provocative and perhaps even condescending from a 21st-century point of view, but if you think of a juste milieu as "a point between two extremes" (RH2), the citation makes better sense. The mean is not intrinsically golden and does not stand *for* something (such as an ideology); it becomes golden by *not* being at the extremities. If there are no extremes to avoid, a golden mean cannot exist. A juste milieu is not a synonym of something that is either good, correct, or right; it is something that is, specifically, not bad but *could* be. It is not (yet another) form of praise; it is a positive sigh of relief that something potentially awful has actually worked out for the best.

AGE

Early 19th century

ETYMOLOGY

The literal translation of the French phrase *juste milieu* is "the right mean" (OED). But *le juste milieu* carries the same "golden" or "optimal" connotation in French as it does in English.

RARITY

Very rare

WHY I LIKE THE PHRASE JUSTE MILIEU

In 1973 Thomas Finkenstaedt and Dieter Wolff published[44] the results of a computerized survey on the origin of about 80,000 words from the third edition of the *Shorter Oxford Dictionary* (OUP, 1944). You may be surprised to learn that the results showed that only 25% of modern English words are derived

from Middle English (and its component languages—chiefly West Germanic
languages and Old Norse). Words directly from Greek only accounted for
about 5.3% of our words, with Latin accounting for a whopping 28.2%. But
(and this sure surprised me) French accounted for a smidgen *more* words, at
28.3%.[45]

So it should be no surprise that among the thousands of English words
derived from French, there is a sizeable group of words (such as **arriviste** and
foudroyant) and phrases (such as juste milieu and **presque vu**) that we have
simply absorbed "as is," without bothering to anglicize.

You will note that, unlike arriviste and foudroyant, juste milieu has neither
an alternative spelling nor pronunciation. While this makes the phrase slightly
less interesting, on a practical level I actually find this lack of choice helpful—
and not just because I am a Libra. Its certainty of pronunciation means that I
can say juste milieu without hesitation, despite my unreliable French accent.

I like this phrase because I like positive achievements and every juste
milieu is exactly that. We may have too much information, but we don't have
enough juste milieux.

❧ JUSTE MILIEU ALIVE

No one was happy about Rosamund's bizarre wedding choices and Bill decided
that, after his success in helping Rosamund to see that Fiji was unaffordable
for many of her friends, he would now attempt to get her to actually change
her mind and select a venue closer to Britain.

"But Rosie, you don't have to discard the romance with the venue. Even
the Caribbean would be better. Or perhaps the **juste milieu** is somewhere
romantic in the Mediterranean. Doesn't Angelo have some family in Italy who
would love to host?"

kalon

{KA-lon. Noun.}

❧ MEANING

The OED defines kalon as "the (morally) beautiful; the ideal good; the 'summum bonum.'"

The W3's definition tells us the source of the word: "the ideal of physical and moral beauty especially as conceived by the philosophers of classical Greece."

Kalon possesses the best of good connotations, so it is no surprise that it is a popular name for people, businesses and brands.

❧ AGE

Mid-18th century

❧ ETYMOLOGY

From the Greek *kalon* (especially in the phrase *to kalon*, "the beautiful"), the neuter of *kalos*, "beautiful."

❧ RARITY

Rare

❧ WHY I LIKE THE WORD KALON

Beauty has become such a commercial quality—something that you buy via fashion, make-up and surgery—that even thinking about the word "kalon" makes me feel good—like the political prisoner smiling at the thought of ideologies that cannot be imprisoned.

Kalon describes a kind of beauty that is more than skin deep and we need more of this kind of beauty or, at least, more recognition of it. Maybe this word can help with that. I very much hope so.

So what might you call a woman who possesses the quality of kalon? By now it will come as no surprise that the French and the Scots have provided us with two wonderful words for this, as they have for so many other situations.

First, from the French, we have a bellibone, pronounced bell-ee-BON(G), "a woman both beautiful and good," adapted from *belle et bonne*, from the Latin *bellus*, "beautiful," and bonus, "good."

And from the Scots? Well, you will actually have to wait because this polysemic ("possessing many meanings") word has an entry all of its own. Now, there's a challenge. Why don't you take a look at the full list of words and try to guess which one it is? You know that it comes after "kalon" in the dictionary, that it means (among other things) beauty and goodness, and that it's a Scots word. So, really, you should be able to pick it or, at the very least, narrow it down to a shortlist of two or three. No pressure. (Sorry, what can I say? I was born to cause trouble.)

To make up for withholding the Scots word, I will give you three more words, all cognates of kalon and all OOO (of obscure origin): kalopsia, "the delusion that things are more beautiful than they actually are"; callipygian, "having beautiful buttocks"; and callimamapygian: "having beautiful breasts and buttocks."

∾ KALON ALIVE

If Jane weren't already married to Bill, she would have proposed to him right now. The clever-clogs had just convinced Rosamund and Angelo to move their wedding to Italy. Now *all* of Rosamund's friends would be able to attend. If only Bill could convince Rosamund to change her fiancé, too, then the world would be perfect! Jane was certain that Angelo would never be right for Rosamund. He adored her physical beauty—the beauty that everyone couldn't help but notice—but there was so much that Jane was sure he didn't fully appreciate. Rosamund had **kalon**, but her goodness often lived in the shadow of her luminous beauty.

karoshi

{kah-ROH-shee. Noun.}

◈ MEANING

The OED (Draft Entry Dec. 2001) thus defines karoshi: "In Japan: death brought on by overwork or job-related exhaustion. Also *attributively*, especially in *karoshi victim*."

A 1990 article from the *Atlanta Journal & Constitution* (C4/5, 23 May) reported that karoshi was "defined as a lethal mix of apoplexy, high blood pressure and stress related to too many hours on the job."

◈ AGE

Late 20th century

◈ ETYMOLOGY

Karoshi is a loanword from Japanese (*karo-shi*, literally "overwork death"), derived from the Chinese characters *ka*, "exceed"; *rou*, "labor"; and *shi*, "death."[46] The OED notes that "the word came into general use in Japan in the late 1980s."

◈ RARITY

Rare

◈ WHY I LIKE THE WORD KAROSHI

Remember our **arriviste**? Let's say he *did* "arrive." He got the job of his dreams, he threw himself into it, working day and night, he made the big bucks, he even earned some respect and eventually threw off the parvenu tag that had doggedly followed him. But then, at 38, karoshi. Dead.

The OED's citations for this word make for particularly sober reading, including this from the Montreal *Gazette* (J6, 4 Feb. 1995): "While the final cause of death in karoshi cases is usually a heart attack, stroke, asthma or suicide, the precipitating causes are psychological. Because of the extreme stresses of overwork, a karoshi victim's body is so disrupted from its normal rhythms that it succumbs to a catastrophic event."

I think karoshi is a powerful word describing an important issue that needs to be more widely discussed and understood. Right across the world the trend has been for people to work more and more hours and this is a trend that we need to reverse, or be prepared to face the escalating consequences. Karoshi is the extreme cost of working to excess, but there is a long list of detrimental effects that typically negate the benefits of that overwork (if there were any), especially if the period of overwork has been a long one. The cost to the worker's health and relationships is well documented, and the impact on productivity (it is so cruel that by working more you often achieve less) is beginning to be properly recognized. But there is another cost one hardly ever hears mentioned: The tragic loss of fun. I say tragic because having fun is a human privilege and to forgo it for stress is, indeed, a tragedy (I speak from experience). As I said, a reversal is required, and I plan to lead the way.

☙ KAROSHI ALIVE

Rosamund asked Jane and Bill if they would both come to Italy a week early to help her with the preparations. Of course they said yes, but now they were saddled with an insanely busy workload to get through before their departure. Jerry was doing an amazing job to help Bill, but the nature of Jane's work meant that there were many tasks she couldn't delegate. Once, while they were brushing their teeth together at one o'clock in the morning, Bill half-joked that they should be careful they didn't end up **karoshi** victims. Jane just looked at him.

kumatage

{koo-mah-TAHZH. Noun.}

⟨~⟩ MEANING

According to *Bowditch's Navigator* (24th edition, 1854), a kumatage is "a bright appearance in the horizon, under the sun or moon, arising from the reflected light of those bodies from the small rippling waves on the surface of the water."

⟨~⟩ AGE

Mid-19th century

⟨~⟩ ETYMOLOGY

From what I can tell, the etymology of this word is unknown, and that can be very exciting, particularly if you think you might have solved the case! Okay, I should be calm; a caveat is definitely required: I am a writer—not an etymologist—and I should probably just stick to reporting etymologies, not trying to second-guess them. So just think of the rest of this section as me thinking out loud (but foolishly writing the thoughts down, publishing them, and opening myself up to all manner of ridicule and embarrassment).

Caveat issued, here is what I found. First I checked for other words starting with kuma-, but found nothing. Next I checked for words starting with cuma- and found the obsolete cumatic, which the OED defines as a "sea-colored blue" (from the Latin *cumatilis*). Naturally this nautical theme piqued my interest, but it was the rest of cumatic's etymology that upped my heart rate: from the Greek *kumat*, "wave." Given that kumatage means "bright appearance [on] small rippling waves," it seemed highly likely (and still does) that the kumat- part of the word was derived from the Greek *kumat*. So that just left the (French) -age, abstract-noun-creating suffix (pronounced AHZH) to be accounted for, and I couldn't see any reason to look past "mirage" for a precedent. Whichever word was coined first, I think they are peas from the same pod. In case you are interested, mirage is derived from the French verb *mirer*, "to be reflected."

ᐰ RARITY
Extremely rare

ᐰ WHY I LIKE THE WORD KUMATAGE

I like the exotic look and sound of kumatage. When I say it I visualise the sight of a kumatage, and that is a very pleasant, soothing and romantic sight. I think of long summer nights, cruising between enticing Greek islands (though I have never actually done that—I get seasick just *looking* at sailboats bobbing about on the water).

The word moonglade is a synonym of kumatage. I think moonglade is another beautiful word. And, derived from German, alpenglow, "the rosy light of the setting or rising sun seen on high mountains" (OED), is another word describing the beauty of the sun's refracted light on some of Earth's topography.

I am sure if I kept looking I would find more examples of man's attempts to define nature's visual masterpieces. If only people would take the time to look up from the screens of their mobile phones they would be able to enjoy so much more of her work.

ᐰ KUMATAGE ALIVE

On their third night in Italy, Bill and Jane enjoyed a romantic seaside dinner to celebrate their ninth wedding anniversary. Only their pocket organizers had saved them from forgetting the day, such was the intensity of the preparations for Rosamund's wedding. But the night had been memorable, first for its ambience, second for the incredible **kumatage** (made even more special by the passage of an ocean liner in front of the sinking sun), and third for the message delivered to them by the maître d'hôtel. Rosamund needed to see Jane, urgently.

lagom

{LAH-gom. Adjective and adverb.}

❧ MEANING

The *Lexin Swedish-English Dictionary* defines *lagom* as "enough, sufficient, adequate, just right."[49] Wikipedia.org notes that: "*lagom* is also widely translated as 'in moderation,' 'in balance,' 'optimal,' 'suitable,' and 'average.' But whereas words like 'sufficient' and 'average' suggest some degree of abstinence, scarcity, or failure, *lagom* carries the connotation of perfection or appropriateness."[50]

So, just as the **juste milieu** is the golden mean, *lagom* is the golden quality or quantity.

❧ AGE

Early 21st century

❧ ETYMOLOGY

According to Wiktionary, *lagom* is a Swedish word (as both an adjective and adverb) that dates back to the 17th century, and is derived from *lag*, "law." Exactly when the word first appeared in English is unclear. I know it featured in Christopher J. Moore's *In Other Words* in 2004, but I would be surprised if that were its first appearance.

Only a small number of English words are from or are derived from Swedish but, as John Alexander points out in *How Swedes Manage*, there are "two other Swedish words related to the lagom concept that have entered English parlance, ombudsman and smörgåsbord." Alexander, who notes that *lagom*'s literal meaning is assumed by most to be something like "according to the law," says that all three words illustrate "the collective spirit of Swedish egalitarianism and fair play." Obviously an ombudsman's role is all about ensuring fairness, but I had never thought about the fact that a smorgasbord will only work if, as Alexander describes, "people queue, and adhere to the rules laid out in the unwritten code book of Swedish social behavior."

❧ RARITY

Very rare

⧫ WHY I LIKE THE WORD LAGOM

There is an unreferenced quote in Wikipedia's *lagom* article that encapsulates the underlying quality represented by *lagom*, which I feel very passionate about: "It's the idea that for everything there is the perfect amount: The perfect, and best, amount of food, space, laughter and sadness."

In the society that I live in the pervading culture is that nothing is ever enough, or good enough. That we *should* always be seeking more when we already have more than enough is, in my opinion, modern Western society's most unecessary failure and most costly habit. From all that I have observed, I cannot see that "more" has made us happier, healthier, more relaxed, or (in real terms) wealthier. Rather, I see stress, obesity, anxiety and social poverty—and yet we largely ignore these deficiencies. Discussing the word *lagom*, and the appreciative and respectful attitude behind it, gives me an opportunity to express my personal dissatisfaction with our collective dissatisfaction with contemporary life, despite its innumerable privileges.

⧫ LAGOM ALIVE

Jane found Rosamund lying on a huge four-poster bed, weeping hysterically into the folds of her crumpled wedding dress. She wanted to postpone the wedding indefinitely, but only if Jane thought that was the right thing to do. "What do you really think?" she sobbed. "Am I just being a complete fool?"

Jane wanted to laugh out loud with joy, but kept her composure. "No, my dear, I think your decision is *lagom*."

lalochezia

{lahl-oh-KEEZ-ee-ə. Noun.}

ᴗ MEANING

Lalochezia is "emotional relief gained by using indecent or vulgar language."[52]

ᴗ AGE

Late 20th century

ᴗ ETYMOLOGY

According to the Online Medical Dictionary,[53] lalochezia is derived from the Greek *lalia*, "speech," and *chezo*, "to relieve oneself." I am unfamiliar with *chezo*, but *lalia* is a combining form that could also be defined as "chatter" or "prattle." A better (perfect, in fact) fit would seem to be the combining form *lalo-*, from *lalos*, which means "prattling, talkative." Both are derived from the verb *lalein*, "to chat, talk."

ᴗ RARITY

Very rare

ᴗ WHY I LIKE THE WORD LALOCHEZIA

I find it reassuring to know that there is a medical term to account for the involuntary utterance of expletives that accompanies dropping your cell phone or sunglasses, especially when you knew only too well that you shouldn't have been holding so many things in your hands or trying to do so many things at the same time.

Lalochezia has the same magical power as water on a child's scratched knee or elbow: it employs a momentary sting to take the sting out of the situation. Just imagine if we *didn't* swear when we stubbed a toe. What would happen to that rush of anger if we didn't quickly curse it out of us? It's like trying to hold in a sneeze—you are likely to burst a blood vessel!

So swearing at yourself or at whatever you just stubbed your toe on is fine with me; swearing at others is not. Oh, I do it every now and then, no question about that, but I am never proud of it.

❧ LALOCHEZIA ALIVE

Most people swear when something bad happens, while others swear between breaths, but Jane Mitchell was neither ordinary nor a celebrity chef; she employed **lalochezia**, in private, to help her celebrate some great achievement that she had worked long and hard for. In her view, cursing wasn't about the words, it was about the gusto with which they were delivered, and tonight she let it rip.

limen

{LAI-mən. Noun.}

℘ MEANING

The OED defines limen as a psychology term meaning: "The limit below which a given stimulus ceases to be perceptible; the minimum amount of stimulus or nerve-excitation required to produce a sensation." It also notes that a limen is also called a threshold.

The adjective is **liminal**.

℘ AGE

Late 19th century

℘ ETYMOLOGY

From the Latin *limen*, "threshold." Both the OED and W3 note that the term was introduced as an equivalent for the German *Schwelle*, a term first used by German psychologist and philosopher Johann Friedrich Herbart in 1824.

Neither dictionary mentions the root of the Latin *limen*, but it would seem highly likely that there is a connection with the word "limit," which has been adapted from the Latin *limes, limit-is*, from *limes*, the word for "boundary," via the French *limite*.

℘ RARITY

Rare

℘ WHY I LIKE THE WORD LIMEN

I will cut straight to the chase: If *limen* is synonymous with *threshold*, why do we need it? I have three reasons.

The first reason is that, while limen and threshold are synonymous in terms of limen's specific psychological meaning, threshold has a wide range of other meanings for which limen is not synonymous.

You can enter a house by passing over a threshold, but not over a limen. You can determine the threshold between productivity and unproductivity, but not the limen. You can pass the threshold of the landing area on a runway, but not its limen. You can pass a tax threshold, but not a tax limen. You can pass the threshold of a stage or an action, but not the limen of either.

So threshold is a well-loaded polyseme and would only benefit from a lighter workload. The W3 listed this short quotation by R. M. Lindner: "make urgent the appetites and needs which are smoldering below the *limen* of awareness." I think limen's freshness and specificity make the phrase just that little bit more effective than if threshold were substituted.

The second reason for bringing limen to life is that its form reminds you of its relationship to subliminal, "below the limen or threshold." We often talk about subliminal messages without any thought for where the limen might lie or what would need to change for the limen to be passed and the message to be perceived. It is curious, really, that we so seldom think about the components of words, so that subliminal is just subliminal, not sub+liminal (limen+al).

And the third reason is that anything that gets us talking about limits and boundaries has to be a good thing. We live as if there were no natural limitations; that anything we can do we should do, and that needs to change.

❧ LIMEN ALIVE

Rosamund was exhausted by travel, by planning for travel, and by planning for the rest of her life, so she asked her very generous Angelo to grant her three more wishes: to forgive her; to let her stay exactly where she was, and not to ask her any questions. Emotions that she had managed to bury for years had broken through the **limen** of her consciousness and she was simply overwhelmed.

logodaedalus

{loh-gə-DEE-də-ləs. Noun; also **logodaedalist**.}

ꙮ MEANING

The OED defines a logodaedalus as "one who is cunning in words." Specifically, the word refers to an "inventor of words" and, as the quotation emphatically states, William Shakespeare set the bar in **logodaedaly**.

Of course, it is almost impossible to know for sure which words Shakespeare actually invented, but here is just a small selection of words whose earliest known usage is in his writings: addiction, courtship, dauntless, discontent, excitements, immediacy, misgiving, pedant, reinforcement, tardiness, watchdog, and zany.[56]

ꙮ AGE

Early 17th century

ꙮ ETYMOLOGY

From the Greek *logodaidalos*, from *logos-*, "word," and *daidalos*, "cunning" or "cunning worker," via Latin.

In Greek mythology, Daedalus was "a most skilful artificer," which means he was a master craftsman. The "cunning" eponym stemmed from him being the master labyrinth creator of his time. There are many versions of his exploits, but they all involve him being incarcerated at Knossos and escaping, with his son Icarus, by flying away using wings he made from feathers, thread and wax.

ꙮ RARITY

Extremely rare

ꙮ WHY I LIKE THE WORD LOGODAEDALUS

Being labeled a logodaedalus is not necessarily a compliment ("*Logodaedaly*, a goodly shew and flourish of Words, without much matter," Nathan Bailey, 1727), but this "colorfulness" is one of the reasons why I like the word.

The equally "colorful" Daedalus myth just adds to the fun, as does Shakespeare's later association with the word: He clearly loved to have fun with words and I am sure he would have loved to have been labeled a logodaedalus.

Being a logodaedalus is not the same thing as being a grandiloquent wordster, or even necessarily an ardent word lover (both labels for which we are well endowed with synonyms), so attempting to keep this entertaining "word word" alive is, I hope, a reasonable indulgence.

❧ LOGODAEDALUS ALIVE

Bill was thrilled for Jane and relieved for Rosamund but, privately, he felt a little bit miffed for himself. Everyone knew that he was quite the **logodaedalus**, especially when it came to speeches, and he had taken the responsibility of speaking on behalf of Jane and Rosamund's father very seriously. He was honored. He would have cried. And he would have had all of the guests crying, too: He had written a real doozie.

lychnobite

{LIK-noh-bite. Noun.}

ᕰᐤ MEANING
The OED defines a lychnobite as "one who turns night into day; a 'fast-liver.'"

ᕰᐤ AGE
Early 18th century

ᕰᐤ ETYMOLOGY
From the Greek *lychnobios*, from *lychnos*, "lamp," and *bios*, "life."

ᕰᐤ RARITY
Extremely rare

ᕰᐤ WHY I LIKE THE WORD LYCHNOBITE
Remember the **arriviste** who suffered **karoshi**? Well, here's one of the ways he will have brought on his premature "departure": working late at night.

Most of us are lychnobites to one degree or another and, at the increasingly growing extremes (such as working or nightclubbing till the early hours of the morning), this lifestyle "costs." You cannot fight the natural rhythms of night and day and expect to avoid paying a physical, mental and social price.

Fighting the night also has an unimaginably high financial cost. We are no longer "burning the midnight oil" of a few table lamps, we are lighting up millions of square miles of cities, suburbs and motorways. A few years ago I saw a composite photograph (by NASA) of Earth's "night-time" sky. The lighting—and light pollution—was staggering. And guess which country blazes brightest? That would be the same country that has a word for "death brought on by overwork": Japan.

We don't *need* to be up all night; we *need* sleep.

And I *need* to mention two closely related (and equally rare) words: the verbs lucubrate and elucubrate. According to the OED, to lucubrate is "(literally) to work by artificial light" or "to produce (literary compositions) by laborious study," and to elucubrate is "to produce (a literary work) by the expenditure of 'midnight oil.'" So, clearly, these two words are both synonymous with "writing anything to a deadline!" Or is that just me?

In case you are interested, both words are derived from Latin, lucubrate from *lucubrat-*, formed from *lucubrare*, formed from *luc-* or *lux*, "light," and elucubrate from *elucubrat-*, formed from *elucubrare*, "to compose by lamplight." They are also both cognates of Lucifer.

And, lastly, wouldn't you assume that The Lychnobite Angling Society had something to do with night-time fishing? All I can say is, read the quotation.

ᏇLYCHNOBITE ALIVE

Bill was always so good at summing up the situation, a talent that Jane valued greatly and slightly hated at the same time.

"You cannot be in two places at once so you will stay and help your sister to get set up and I will return to work. And when you return to work you will not become a **lychnobite** and half-kill yourself—your clients will simply have to wait. Rosie needs you now, your clients think they need you 'yesterday,' but I need you for all my tomorrows."

maieutic

{may-YOO-tik or mai-YOO-tik. Adjective; also **maieutical**.}

ᓚ MEANING

The W3 defines maieutic as "of or relating to the dialectic method practiced by Socrates in order to elicit and clarify the ideas of others." The RH2 takes things a step further by also defining the method: ". . . by interrogation and insistence on close and logical reasoning." And the OED (Draft Revision June 2000) adds the purpose: ". . . assisting a person to become fully conscious of ideas previously latent in the mind."

The (plural) noun is **maieutics**.

ᓚ AGE

Mid-17th century

ᓚ ETYMOLOGY

From the Greek *maieutikos*, literally "midwifery" or "obstetrics," from *maieuesthai*, "to serve as a midwife," from *maia*, "midwife" and *-tikos*, a suffix used to form adjectives from verbs.

ᓚ RARITY

Very rare

ᓚ WHY I LIKE THE WORD MAIEUTIC

Maieutic questioning is my thing—it is what I try to do with my writing and teaching—and this is the reason I chose the word.

Maieutics is "based on the idea that the truth is latent in the mind of every human being due to his innate reason but has to be 'given birth' by answering questions (or problems) intelligently proposed."[59] To embrace maieutic techniques it seems to me that you need to be an egalitarian: You need to believe that everyone has equal ownership of the truth before expending energy trying to help them to access it. This is who I am and uncovering hidden potential is what motivates me—it floats my boat.

My observations tell me that we *are* all substantively the same, and I want to say that I "know" that this is so, but because I do not *know* everybody (or possibly anybody), I can only say that I "believe" we are so. I do know that we *appear* different; for observable reasons we act differently and treat each other differently, but when I ask the right (maieutic) questions, I am able to show people that our underlying motivations are the same, that we are all intelligent in our own way, and that we are all equally important and unimportant.

As Socrates and Plato deduced, by questioning one another we best equip ourselves to recognize our place in the world and execute our shared responsibilities within it. We can also inspire each other to do great things, and we can help each other to avoid and alleviate stresses and concerns.

❧ MAIEUTIC ALIVE

Angelo had returned to Chicago to oversee the opening of his new clinic and pack up their few American possessions (and, Jane wondered, to do who knew what else). But the time that Jane had alone with Rosamund was precious and both sisters instinctively endeavored to make it count. They talked and talked and Jane tried her best to ask helpful, **maieutic** questions that no one else would ask of Rosamund, while Rosamund did her very best to answer them.

mancinism

{MAN(T)-sə-niz-əm. Noun.}

๏ MEANING

The W3 defines mancinism as "the condition of being left-handed." While I applaud the crispness of this definition, the OED's treatment (Draft Revision Sept. 2000), "the state or condition of having a bias in some way towards the left-hand side of the body," has the advantage of embracing a range of other left-hand side tendencies, such as left-footedness.

๏ AGE

Late 19th century

๏ ETYMOLOGY

From the Italian *mancinismo*, from *mancino*, from *manco*, "lacking," and *-ino*, *-ine* ("pertaining to"), and *-ismo*, ism. So a literal translation of mancinism could be "lackingness." And if you further consider its Latin root (*mancus*, "having a useless hand, maimed, crippled, feeble, powerless," from *manus*, "hand" and *-cus*, which the OED describes as a "suffix forming adjectives apparently associated with physical defects"), it could be "defective-handedness."

๏ RARITY

Extremely rare

๏ WHY I LIKE THE WORD MANCINISM

Though the unequal treatment of people based on something as meaningless as handedness is historical in most places today, it is far from obsolete. My own mother was encouraged (with a ruler) to use her right hand rather than her naturally dominant left. And in etymological terms there is a significant history of inequality in words for handedness that must rival even black and white as unequally "loaded" lexical pairs.

So, we have left and right. Left has few negative connotations (unless you are a staunch conservative) and no positive ones; right has no negative ones (unless you are a staunch socialist) and many highly significant positive ones: correctness, morality, truth, justice, authority, title.

Then we have sinister and dexter, "on the left-hand side" and "on the right-hand side." Sinister has 12 main definitions in the OED of which only the last four are actually about the left side. Of the remaining eight, here are just a few highlights: deceive, mislead, prejudice, malice, ill-will, adverse, unfavorable, darkly suspicious, dishonest, unfair, underhand, dark, corrupt, evil, bad, base, erring, erroneous, indicating misfortune or disaster, inauspicious, mischief, and harmful.

Dexter, on the other hand (sorry, I couldn't resist), has just two main definitions comprising seven sub-definitions. All but one are about the right side, and the (obsolete) exception: "Of omens: Seen or heard on the right side; hence, auspicious, favorable, propitious." Of course, if we look at dextrous the connotations are (almost) all good. Again, the highlights: handy, convenient, suitable, fitting, deft or nimble of hand, neat-handed, skilful, mental adroitness, expert, clever. The negative connotations: "In a bad sense: 'Clever,' crafty, cunning."

So, given that the scales are already so heavily tipped in favor of "the right," why would we want another prejudice-laden word like mancinism for left-handedness? For the dogs and cats, of course, and all those other animals that don't have hands.

～ MANCINISM ALIVE

Jane and Rosamund were decorating Rosamund's new bedroom. As Rosamund placed a few personal things on the right-hand bedside table Jane became confused. "Didn't you always used to sleep on the left?"

"Yes, but I *can* sleep on the right, Angelo can't. I suppose it is some sort of **mancinism**, but it really doesn't bother me in the slightest."

millihelen

{MIL-ə-hel-ən. Noun.}

ᗊ MEANING

According to Wiktionary, a millihelen is: "(*informal*) A unit of measure of pulchritude, corresponding to the amount of beauty required to launch one ship."[61] The entry also includes an important usage note: "According to Raymond Augustine Bauer and Kenneth J. Gergen (*The Study of Policy Formation*, 1968), 'one could also speak of fractional millihelens, say, enough beauty to launch two cabin boys.'"

Wikipedia's article on humorous units of measurement notes that "negative values have also been observed—these, of course, are measured by the number of ships sunk or the number of clocks stopped."[62]

ᗊ AGE

Mid-20th century

ᗊ ETYMOLOGY

From Wiktionary: "From the SI prefix milli- (indicating a thousandth) + Helen, of Troy, the maiden so beautiful that her abduction by Paris sparked the Trojan War and was said, in Christopher Marlowe's 1604 *Tragical History of Doctor Faustus*, to have 'launched a thousand ships.'"

Exactly who coined the term (and thus created the measurement) is uncertain, but the two leading candidates are Cambridge mathematician W. A. H. Rushton and well-known science-fiction writer Isaac Asimov.

ᗊ RARITY

Extremely rare

ᗊ WHY I LIKE THE WORD MILLIHELEN

This is a word that positively exudes a *by*-nerdy-scientists-*for*-nerdy-scientists aura, but it has caught on, at least a bit. For example, there is a mildly risqué web site (millihelens.com) devoted to measuring the millihelen rating of both men and women. The source of the photographs can only ever be dubious, and most of the photos of the highly-rated girls are titillating (and I don't mean ticklish), but the system for rating them is pure science.

Beauty, as the saying goes, is in the eye of the beholder, and this means that if you rate beauty on a scale—whether that scale is 1-to-10 or 1-to-1000—you can never know if your 8-out-of-10 is the same as your buddy's 8-out-of-10. So the web site tackles this by using comparisons (and at least 10 of them) to calculate ratings. Their "simple explanation" of this "is that the score in millihelens (abbreviated mH) is related to the win/loss ratio of the picture, but [is] also dependent on the scores of all the other pictures." Their "complicated explanation" (and it sounds impressive to me) "is that the site places all of the pictures on a normal distribution and assigns scores based on distance from the mean." I suspect W. A. H. Rushton and Isaac Asimov would both approve.

Millihelen is an example of a nonce word (one invented for a particular occasion) that has taken a foothold in the lexicon. Here are two others that get my vote: Earthlubber (*You haven't been in space yet?*); and ombibulous, "the manner of a **bleezy** person who drinks anything at all." And, lastly, one that has already flourished and doesn't need my vote: retrosexual, "the antithesis of the metrosexual: a man with an undeveloped aesthetic sense who spends as little time and money as possible on his appearance and lifestyle."[63]

⌒ MILLIHELEN ALIVE

The drudgery of returning to work was briefly mitigated for Bill by a record-breaking debut on their office "Wikihelen." The new barista from the office building's café debuted with a whopping 882 **millihelens**, pushing Sandy from the dry-cleaners off the top spot for the first time in 24 weeks.

nihil obstat

{nai-hil-OHB-stat or ni-hil-OHB-stat. Noun.}

❧ MEANING

The W3 has two definitions for nihil obstat: "1. the certification by an official censor of the Roman Catholic Church that a book has been examined and found to contain nothing opposed to faith and morals. 2. authoritative or official approval." It illustrates the second definition with this brief quotation: "the surest road to fame was . . . through the imprimatur and *nihil obstat* of a foreign critic—P. H. Odegard."

❧ AGE

Late 19th century

❧ ETYMOLOGY

Nihil obstat is Latin for "nothing hinders." Or "nothing stands in [your] way." Or "nothing obstructs."

❧ RARITY

Rare

❧ WHY I LIKE THE PHRASE NIHIL OBSTAT

I was already a fan of a number of Latin phrases (see below), but this one is new to me and it possesses both a gusto and (to use Latin again) a gravitas that turns the mid-range sedan of nothing hinders into the snub-nosed sports car of nihil obstat. I can just see Bruce Willis ending an appropriately short and inspiring speech to his platoon of marines (who are about to parachute their way into a "secure facility" to rescue the one person in the world who can produce a vaccine for a new, highly contagious killer virus) with a gravelly, "Nihil obstat boys, nihil obstat," to which they all reply with a macho, chest-thumping "Hooah!" before doing the business and saving us all.

Okay, three more (hooah!) Latin phrases.

First, ignotum per ignotius: "An attempt to explain what is obscure by something which is more obscure, leading to 'confusion worse confounded' (OED).

Second, rara avis: "1. A person of a type seldom encountered; an exceptional person, a paragon . . . 2. That which is seldom found; an unusual occurrence, etc.; something very remarkable. 3. literally, a rare bird" (OED). Such a person might well also be a **cynosure**.

And last, sub rosa, a phrase which has become significantly better known through *The Da Vinci Code* (both the book and the film): "'under the rose' . . . used in English to connote secrecy or confidentiality"[65] (Wikipedia).

⟅ NIHIL OBSTAT ALIVE

For reasons no one was able to explain, the Biggswater Business House Fun Run had of its own accord evolved into a big deal. Bill was a team captain and it was time for his final pep talk. He could overhear other team captains trying to rally their motley crews with a limp "let's win this thing" or a mildly hopeful "come on, we can do it." But Bill knew his dream team of speedy brainiacs would respond to something altogether different and so he urged them to success with a resolute gaze and a steely, **"Nihil obstat."**

nikhedonia

{naik-he-DOH-nee-ə. Noun.}

ᗌ MEANING
According to the Word Information web site[66], nikhedonia is "the pleasure of anticipating victory or success."[67]

ᗌ AGE
Late 20th century

ᗌ ETYMOLOGY
From Nike, the Greek goddess of victory, and the Greek *hëdonë*, "pleasure."

This word is OUO (of unknown origin), but I think the quotation goes a long way to confirming its legitimacy. There is also a precedent in anhedonia: "inability to feel pleasure" (OED).

ᗌ RARITY
Extremely rare

ᗌ WHY I LIKE THE WORD NIKHEDONIA
Nikhedonia is presumably what distinguishes slow-and-steady plodders from go-getters: both are ambitious, both are motivated, but only the go-getters really take pleasure in the ride.

I used to say that if I could change anything in my life, I wouldn't, because that might mean my relationships were poorer, or non-existent. But since having children I have changed my tune: I would just try to have more fun, and I guess nikhedonia would be a part of that.

I have always derived great pleasure from the anticipation of travel. In fact, the preparation can sometimes be more satisfying than the travel itself—it certainly lasts much longer and it is exceedingly better value for money. But, as for other aspects of life—for my work, in particular—I have been a plodder. Even now, I am still incapable of nikhedonia because I simply don't know what the feast of success tastes like or, indeed, if I truly deserve to be invited to the table. I have but nibbled on the hors d'œuvres (and very tasty they have been).

Back to anticipating travel. I don't travel anywhere near enough these days but, when I do, I still love the research and planning. For me, travel and experiences and having fun *is* success because being successful earns you money and buys you time, options, and expensive vacations.

❧ NIKHEDONIA ALIVE

Bill's company had been aggressively recruiting over the past year and two of the new recruits just happened to be top-class marathoners. As Bill approached the finish line of the Biggswater Business House Fun Run, he smiled with **nikhedonia**, knowing that those two runners, along with the three very fit runners he already had on the team, had all long since completed the race. Only the times of the first five runners in any team counted and he was darn near certain that they had won first prize.

noosphere

{NOH-ə-sfeeə or NOH-ə-sfee(ə)r. Noun.}

ᛢᛚ MEANING

The OED (Draft Revision Dec. 2003) defines this somewhat esoteric concept as: "the part of the biosphere occupied by thinking humanity; specially . . . a stage or sphere of evolutionary development characterized by (the emergence or dominance of) consciousness, the mind, and interpersonal relationships, postulated as following the stage of the establishment of human life. Also figuratively."

Wikipedia's article for noosphere ("the sphere of thought") explains its evolutionary context: "In the original theory of [Ukrainian-Russian mineralogist and geochemist, Vladimir] Vernadsky, the noosphere is the third in a succession of phases of development of the Earth, after the geosphere (inanimate matter) and the biosphere (biological life). Just as the emergence of life fundamentally transformed the geosphere, the emergence of human cognition fundamentally transforms the biosphere."[68]

The adjective is **noospheric**.

ᛢᛚ AGE

Early 20th century

ᛢᛚ ETYMOLOGY

From the French *noösphère*, formed from the Greek *noos* or *nous*, "mind" (think "using your nous"), and the French *sphère*, after the French *biosphère*.

ᛢᛚ RARITY

Rare

ᛢᛚ WHY I LIKE THE WORD NOOSPHERE

I have always been fascinated by anthropology, evolution and philosophy— Who are we? Where have we come from? Why are we here?—so, for me, the concept of a noosphere is like a supergroup of related interests and I am very excited about hearing them play together.

The aspect of the noosphere that fascinates me most is its conception:

the point in evolution when consciousness developed. Remember the famous philosophical statement by René Descartes—*Cogito, ergo sum* ("I think, therefore I am")—well, this moment is what he was writing about. Consciousness is a switch that, once on, would (and will) never be switched off. For our species, it has been a tremendous opportunity as well as a tremendous burden, and I really don't think we understand its effects well enough. Discussions about the noosphere can only help to fill this deficit.

⌒ NOOSPHERE ALIVE

Jane's newest client was an eccentric superyacht owner who wanted his cabin redecorated for his wife's birthday in 10 days" time. Just the pressure she didn't need. To make things worse, his brief was for the room's décor to represent a "primeval awakening." She had no idea what that meant. She called Bill.

"You mean the **noosphere**?" Bill prompted.

"Do I?"

"Could be. The evolution of human consciousness sounds like 'primeval awakening' to me. I'd ask him about his views on religion—that ought to give you a few more clues."

offing

{OFF-ing. Noun.}

♋ MEANING
From the RH2:

1. the more distant part of the sea seen from the shore, beyond the anchoring ground.
2. a position at a distance from shore.
3. (*idiom*) in the offing,
   a. at a distance but within sight.
   b. in the projected future; likely to happen.

Offing also performs a cautionary role. The OED notes that the offing is "a position . . . beyond in-shore navigational dangers" and the W3's definition includes "a position or course near to but safely clear of the land," citing a quote by S. E. Morison that indicates such a position would be "a good offing."

♋ AGE
Early 17th century

♋ ETYMOLOGY
Offing is simply a compound of off and the suffix -ing.

♋ RARITY
Rare

♋ WHY I LIKE THE WORD OFFING
We all know what "in the offing" means, but isn't it satisfying to know what an offing actually is? If someone had asked me what an offing was prior to my researching this book, the best answer I could have offered was "a noun."

That said, I did not choose the word because it unlocked the key to a saying; I chose it because the offing is a part of the physical world we live in and I want this word in my geographical vocabulary. Beach, shoreline, foreshore, offshore, offing, horizon. Not knowing it is like **not knowing that** between the earth and space there is not just "the atmosphere," but the troposphere, stratosphere and so on through to the exosphere, whose "atoms and molecules escape into space."[70]

And offing also provides me with a valuable metaphorical tool. Consider this: "a waiter hovered in the offing," which the W3 used to illustrate offing's meaning of "in the near distance."

I think this word is a little gem well worth rescuing, particularly given that it may one day play some small role in assisting me to avoid fog, rocks, anchored vessels, and other nautical dangers.

⌒ OFFING ALIVE

Jane was standing alone in the master bedroom of her client's superyacht at Southampton. She was waiting for the client, and for inspiration. Through the bedroom's floor-to-ceiling stern-facing window she could see one of P&O's huge passenger liners in dock—its outline reminding her of the ship she and Bill had seen in the **offing** that eventful night in Italy.

omnist

{OM-nist. Noun.}

ᴖ MEANING

The W3 provides the characteristically succinct "one that believes in all religions," which is interesting because the OED's definition (Draft Revision June 2004) indicates that an omnist could also be "a person who believes in a single transcendent purpose or cause uniting all things or people, or the members of a particular group of people."

Wikipedia's article on omnism refers to the fact that "modern day self-described 'omnists' . . . have rediscovered and begun to redefine the term . . . to refer more to an acceptance of the legitimacy of all religions."[71]

ᴖ AGE

Mid-19th century

ᴖ ETYMOLOGY

From the Latin *omnis*, "all," and the agent-noun-forming suffix -ist.

ᴖ RARITY

Extremely rare

ᴖ WHY I LIKE THE WORD OMNIST

Some people are of "no fixed abode"; I am of "no fixed religion." This is not to say that I am not religious—in many ways I am—but I simply cannot bear to house what I believe and feel in something fixed and historical. For me, it is not a matter of faith (I believe in plenty of "things" I cannot see), it is a matter of logic.

Whether a supreme being exists or not is simply not something I feel I need to have a view on, so I am neither an atheist nor an agnostic (I don't know where to draw the line between what is knowable and unknowable). I cannot believe in "God" because if I did I would also have to become a member of an organized religion and, by doing that, my faith would require me to suddenly have a view on everyone else's religion or supreme being. In short, I would have to think that they were wrong and I was right.

So you can see why omnism is of great interest to me. I am *nearly* a humanist, but humanism is overtly atheistic so it's not a perfect fit. Omnism, on the other hand, allows me to "believe in all religions," or just their legitimacy, and/or "a single transcendent purpose or cause uniting all things or people." Like all those "modern day self-described 'omnists' . . . [who] have rediscovered and begun to redefine the term," I need a malleable -ism and this one is as accommodating as a chameleon's skin. So, the next time someone asks me if I am an atheist or an agnostic I will take delight in letting them know that I am an omnist. And when they ask me what that is I'll just make something up.

❦ OMNIST ALIVE

Following Bill's suggestion, Jane easily turned her conversation with the superyacht owner to the topic of religion and he turned out to be an **omnist**. In explaining what this actually meant to him, he inadvertently gave Jane the inspiration she had been missing. Bill was spot-on. Now, all she needed to do was turn her ideas into a newly decorated room in just over a week.

omnistrain

{OM-nee-streyn. Noun.}

✒ MEANING

In his book *There's a Word for It!: A Grandiloquent Guide to Life*, Charles Harrington Elster defines omnistrain as "the stress of trying to cope with everything at once (otherwise known as everyday life)."[73]

✒ AGE

Late 20th century

✒ ETYMOLOGY

This is another OOO (of obscure origin) word (I have no clues as to where Elster found it),[74] but it is obviously a compound of the combining form, omni-, "all," and strain.

✒ RARITY

Extremely rare

✒ WHY I LIKE THE WORD OMNISTRAIN

This neologism does not yet appear in the OED but, interestingly, if it did, it would be the very next word after omnist. Given that the OED has more than 230,000 words, I would have to compile another 2,299 lists of 100 words before I could expect this to happen again.

But I digress. I like the word omnistrain because it describes reality.

Typically, with every new gadget and media format that we invent, we add more stress and strain to our lives, not less. This is because, as consumers, we usually add or upgrade and seldom reduce or refine. If you do this enough (and almost all of us do), your possessions begin to overwhelm you, and this translates into stress.

Great, you just treated yourself to a jetski on "the plastic." Now it just has to be transported, fueled, insured, stored, maintained, actually paid for, and actually used. When you do find time to use it, you then have to endure the entirely justified disapproval of all the people whose peace and quiet you have just shattered with the piercing, high-pitched drone of your purposeless, fossil fuel–burning toy. If only they had been privileged enough to enjoy with you the incredible thrill of zipping backward and forward, backward and forward, then they might not be so grumpy. But as it is, your personal thrill (which could be achieved with as little effort, and benefit, as sticking your head out the window of your car as you drive to work) creates a whole lot more displeasure than pleasure.

But I **divagate**. The reality of human activity is that when you juggle work or play, stress increases and enjoyment diminishes. Potentially **ambrosial** meals become everyday meals when they are interrupted by: TV programs, phone calls, text messages, or sorry-I-just-need-to's. Our **arriviste** will have almost certainly been a "juggler"; our **ataraxic** (the peaceful, *living* person) will almost certainly not be a "juggler."

This word may be obscure but it sure gets my vote. I hope people use the word, recognize the issue, and end up with some spare time so they can learn how to juggle balls (it's entertaining and very therapeutic), not jobs and junk.

❦ OMNISTRAIN ALIVE

After two months of catching up on work after Rosamund's aborted wedding, Bill and Jane were both suffering from **omnistrain** and desperately needed a break. So Bill booked them into a romantic boutique hotel just outside Bath for a long weekend of doing absolutely nothing.

pandiculation

{pan-dik-yoo-LEY-shən. Noun.}

❧ MEANING

The W3 defines pandiculation as "a stretching and stiffening, especially of the trunk and extremities (as when fatigued and drowsy or after waking from sleep)."

The adjective is **pandiculated**.

❧ AGE

Early 17th century

❧ ETYMOLOGY

From the Latin *pandiculat-*, from *pandiculari*, "to stretch oneself" (from *pandere*, "to stretch, unfold"), via French.

❧ RARITY

Very rare

❧ WHY I LIKE THE WORD PANDICULATION

In many cultures stretching for exercise is a central and keenly anticipated part of daily life, but for the rest of us stretching our muscles is just something we do to warm up and attempt to avoid injury. So that's one kind of stretching.

The essential and involuntary stretching that we luxuriate in when waking is, I say, an altogether different kind of stretching and it deserves a word of its own—pandiculation.

There is something fundamentally wrong with waking up so abruptly that you are out of bed and into your morning ablutions *sans* pandiculation. Those few minutes of waking *in bed* are a daily gift that we should always enjoy and treasure. The moment of pandiculation is really one of life's joys and to forgo it to be at the office five minutes earlier is a very poor trade indeed. Just ask any cat.

Of course, stretching at the end of the day, when you are tired and ready for bed, is also pandiculation and it can also be an absolute delight, as long as you don't fight it. Suppressing pandiculation and the accompanying yawn is, again, an unwise and fruitless choice. The best option is to submit and let your body transition you from wakefulness to sleepiness in the most natural manner possible.

But don't take my word for it—listen to the doctor. (That means read the quotation.)

❧ PANDICULATION ALIVE

This was the best idea Bill had had in a very long time. They slept in and eventually wandered into town for brunch at about 11 o'clock. Neither wanting to break the lazy spell that hung over them, they decided to head back to the hotel to veg out, read newspapers, magazines, maybe even pick up a novel. But much to their surprise, within an hour they were both napping. Bill woke first and was glad he did because he loved to watch Jane asleep in the daytime when you could really see her. And when she woke, her **pandiculation** was a joy to behold.

papilionaceous

{pə-pil-ee-ə-NEY-shəs. Adjective.}

ᕰ᠍ MEANING

The W3 has two closely related but distinct definitions for papilionaceous. The first, derived from *papilio* (Latin for "butterfly"), is "resembling a butterfly; specifically: irregular and suggestive of a butterfly in shape." This definition is illustrated with the phrase, *the corolla of many leguminous plants is papilionaceous.* The second definition, derived from the Latin botanical term *Papilionaceae*, is "of or relating to the family Leguminosae."

And, just in case you were wondering, a corolla (not the car) is "the whorl of leaves (petals) either separate or grown together, forming the inner envelope of the flower, and generally its most conspicuous part; usually 'colored' (i.e., not green), and of delicate texture" (OED) and examples from the family Leguminosae are the sweet pea, bean, vetch, and clover.

So what the definitions are really saying is that there is a family of plants (commonly known as legumes) whose flowers resemble the shape of a butterfly.

ᕰ᠍ AGE

Late 17th century

ᕰ᠍ ETYMOLOGY

From the Latin *papilio (papilionis)*, "butterfly," and the suffix -aceous, "of the nature of."

ᕰ᠍ RARITY

Very rare

ᕰ᠍ WHY I LIKE THE WORD PAPILIONACEOUS

Papilionaceous is a great-sounding word and is worth promoting for that reason alone, but I have actually chosen it for a different reason. Just as **glandaceous** reminds us that there are many more words for colors than the primary and secondary staples we typically employ, papilionaceous will, I hope, serve as a

I am well aware that many readers will exclaim—"It is not the common practice of English baronets to remit half a year's rent to their tenants for poetry, or for any thing else." This may be very true; but I have found a character in the Rambler, No. 82, who made a very different bargain, and who says, "And as Alfred received the tribute of the Welsh in wolves' heads, I allowed my tenants to pay their rents in butterflies, till I had exhausted the **papilionaceous** tribe. I then directed them to the pursuit of other animals, and obtained, by this easy method, most of the grubs and insects which land, air, or water can supply . . . I have, from my own ground, the longest blade of grass upon record, and once accepted, as a half year's rent for a field of wheat, an ear, containing more grains than had been seen before upon a single stem."

Robert Bloomfield, *Mayday with the Muses* (1822)

reminder that there are many more shapes than round, oval, and the standard set of straight-sided shapes from triangle through to dodecahedron.

Here are just three of what else is offered. Lunette: "the figure or shape of a crescent moon" (W3). Muriform: "composed of cells that are arranged in a regular fashion, like bricks in a wall" (OED). Obrotund: "of a rounded form, but longer in one direction than in the other; somewhat round" (OED).

And for something shifty that seems to change shape before your very eyes? Try protean: "readily assuming different forms or characters; extremely variable" from Proteus, "a sea god . . . noted for his ability to assume different forms" (RH2).

⁶ PAPILIONACEOUS ALIVE

Bill was loving being away from the city and wanted something tangible to remind him of the feeling. He took Jane to a quaint little antique shop away from the main tourist area and bought her a delightful French brooch. It was **papilionaceous**, the "wings" appearing to flutter as the light danced on delicate pink and crimson crystals.

paralipsis

{pa-rə-LIP-sis. Noun; also **paraleipsis**, **paralepsis**.}

ᖰᕼ MEANING

The OED (Draft Revision Dec. 2007) defines paralipsis as: "the rhetorical device of emphasising or drawing attention to something by professing to say little or nothing about it, or affecting to dismiss it (usually with such phrases as *not to mention, to say nothing of,* etc.); an instance of this."

The RH2 definition takes a slightly different tack, focusing on the omission rather than on the description of that omission: "the suggestion, by deliberately concise treatment of a topic, that much of significance is being omitted, as in 'not to mention other faults.'"

Either way, a paralipsis is a pretty sneaky figure of speech.

ᖰᕼ AGE

Mid-16th century

ᖰᕼ ETYMOLOGY

From the Greek *paraleipsis,* "an omission," from *paraleipein,* "to leave on one side" (which comprises the prefix *para-,* "beside," and *leipein,* "to leave"), and *-sis,* via Latin.

ᖰᕼ RARITY

Very rare

ᖰᕼ WHY I LIKE THE WORD PARALIPSIS

I have specifically chosen paralipsis as an example of a rhetorical device, and I specifically want to highlight rhetorical devices in order to illustrate that employing them (manipulating each other through our choice of words and phrases) is neither unusual nor necessarily dodgy, it is just what we do.

Rhetoric is essentially the art of "persuasion" through the use of language. Persuasion can take many forms, including education, inspiration, and enlightenment. A rhetorical device is just "a technique that an author or speaker uses to evoke an emotional response in his audience,"[77] this being the most effective way to engage and involve an audience.

. . . Gore has now laid the groundwork to claim victory was stolen from him—which is exactly what he did in that clever bit of **paralipsis** on CBS' "60 Minutes" Sunday. If George W. Bush is inaugurated on Jan. 20, Gore said, he'll be my president, too, and I'll never accuse him of stealing the election.

Linda Chavez, "The Gig is Up,"
Jewish World Review, 5 Dec. 2000[78]

So that's the context of paralipsis; now to the specifics. I assure you it is unlikely that a day has passed in your adult life when you have not employed a paralipsis. Every time you say "not to mention" you are using one, though not forcefully (precisely because that particular turn of phrase is so common). To create a successful (forceful) paralipsis you need to be sure of your goal, which will usually be to soften the blow of fair criticism (to make it more palatable, thus increasing the chance of it being heard and acted upon) or to distance yourself from unfair criticism that you still want to make. *I don't want to even mention anything about the state you left the house in this morning.*

Now that you are aware of paralipsis, you will probably find that you regularly catch authors, politicians, and your family and friends using the device.

⟋ PARALIPSIS ALIVE
Jane and Bill thought they might eat at a bistro recommended in the local newspaper, but were put off by the hotel manager whose **paralipsis** was about as subtle as a sledgehammer: "Oh yes, a delightful establishment, though I shall say nothing at all of the recent incident with the mistakenly labeled rat poison."

paraph

{PA-raf or pə-RAF. Noun and verb.}

ᕫᕫ MEANING

The OED (Draft Revision Dec. 2007) and the RH2 both define a paraph (the noun) as "a flourish made after a signature, originally as a precaution against forgery."

The OED also notes that a paraph used to mean what we today call a paragraph.

ᕫᕫ AGE

Late 16th century

ᕫᕫ ETYMOLOGY

In the sense of "a flourish made after a signature," possibly from the Middle French *paraphe, paraffe*, "abbreviated signature," or the Latin *paraphus*. In the sense of "paragraph," possibly from the French *paragraphe*, or from the Latin *paragraphus*.

ᕫᕫ RARITY

Very rare

ᕫᕫ WHY I LIKE THE WORD PARAPH

English is a remarkably well-endowed language. To be fair, it doesn't have a word for absolutely everything (for example, what is the word for the anticipation of missing someone?), but it does have at least one word for nearly everything, including this left-hand page (a verso), and that right-hand page (a recto), "the line behind which a player must stand when throwing darts" (an oche),[79] and "a spike for holding a candle" (a pricket).[80]

So I should not have been in the slightest bit surprised that there is also a word for the flourish with which you may or may not embellish your signature. But I was surprised, pleasantly surprised.

Knowledge is a treasure to be enjoyed repeatedly. Knowing what a paraph is will forever enhance my experiences of looking at important old documents (which, as you will have probably guessed, I love to do) because paraphs regularly feature. And I highly recommend looking at some famous examples of paraphs. Two that I know you can see on Wikipedia are those of John Hancock (from the United States Declaration of Independence), whose signature was "famous for its bold paraph,"[81] and the even more embellished triple-paraphed signature of Elizabeth I.[82]

The definitions of a paraph all mention that it can be (and was) used "as a sort of rude safeguard against forgery" (W3), but I suspect that the primary motivation was simply to impress people—the size and intricacy of your paraph (or, indeed, paraphs) an indicator of your standing in society. Perhaps it is time I upgraded my own signature—but just to foil the forgers, you understand.

∾ PARAPH ALIVE

Bill decided he wanted a keepsake of their long weekend for himself. He returned to the same antique shop where he had bought Jane's brooch and searched through a shelf of first editions before turning to a large cabinet full of rare documents. In the cabinet he found a letter signed, with modest **paraph**, by C. L. Dodgson—a man much better known by his pseudonym, Lewis Carroll. It was expensive—but what a treasure.

peccable

{PEHK-ə-bəl. Adjective.}

❧ MEANING

This is an interesting word and the definitions are all short, so it is worth visiting all three.

OED (Draft Revision Dec. 2005): "1. Capable of sinning; liable to sin. In later use also (frequently in humorous contrast to impeccable): fallible, imperfect, flawed. 2. Sinful, wrong. *Obsolete. Rare.*"

RH2: "liable to sin and error."

W3: "liable or prone to sin: susceptible to temptation."

The noun is **peccability**.

❧ AGE

Early 17th century

❧ ETYMOLOGY

From the Latin *peccabilis*, from *peccare*, "to sin," via French.

❧ RARITY

Very rare

❧ WHY I LIKE THE WORD PECCABLE

As with **divagate**, peccable highlights the gap of bias between aspiration and actuality. In this case, the sphere is human nature rather than human behavior, but the gap is just as wide.

If you think about it, does any of us know anyone who is *incapable* of sin and error? Jesus is an obvious candidate (though whether he couldn't sin or just didn't sin appears to be unclear), but the rest of us are unequivocally peccable. And yet which adjective is around 300 times more popular?

How can impeccability be so disproportionately popular? My guess is that, having found the idea of being described as impeccable quite agreeable, we simply expanded its meaning to include something like "faultless," which we could then apply to specific behavior. *His attitude is impeccable.* Conversely, the disagreeable nature of peccability meant that we didn't bother to even things up by expanding its meaning at the same time.

So peccable and impeccable are unbalanced antonyms, both in terms of popularity and the scope of their meaning. A very similar example is nocent ("harmful, guilty") and innocent. And a pair whose meanings are balanced but whose popularity certainly isn't is nocuous ("noxious, hurtful") and innocuous.

As you can see, the "positive" twin usually wins the popularity stakes, but not always: we don't often return from a concert discussing how ruly ("obedient, orderly") the crowd was.

⌒ PECCABLE ALIVE

Jerry Johnson was **peccable** after all. Bill had asked him to be his stand-in at an early morning meeting in Paris on Monday and, well, he slept through it. To avoid any chance of missing the meeting through delayed flights he had traveled to Paris on Sunday and, according to Bill's secretary, he entertained someone the night before who, during the night, had relieved him of his wallet and his nifty little travel alarm clock.

peregrinate

{PER-i-grə-neyt. Adjective and verb.}

MEANING

As an adjective, the OED (Draft Revision Dec. 2007) defines peregrinate as "*Chiefly literary*. Influenced by or affecting foreign styles or expressions; affected; mannered. Also: having the appearance of a foreigner; outlandish." A second definition states: "of or relating to pilgrimage or pilgrims." The W3 defines the adjective simply as "having the air of one who has traveled or lived abroad: foreign," and the RH2 doesn't list the adjective at all.

As an intransitive verb (that is, a verb that can stand by itself without an object), to peregrinate is "to travel; journey; to go from place to place" or "to reside abroad" (OED, Draft Revision Dec. 2005). The RH2 qualifies its entry with "especially to walk on foot" and, interestingly, the W3 only lists the pedestrian meaning: "to travel on foot: walk, tour."

Accordingly, when it gives the meaning of the word as a transitive verb, the W3 maintains its pedestrian-only position with "to walk over: traverse," while the RH2 maintains its buck-each-way position with "to travel or journey, especially to walk on foot," and the OED bets against singling out the pedestrian mode of transport with "to travel along, across, or around; to traverse."

The noun is **peregrinity**. A **peregrinator** is a "traveler," "wanderer," or "pilgrim."

AGE

Late 16th century

ETYMOLOGY

From the Latin *peregrinatus*, "having traveled or sojourned abroad," from *peregrinari*, "to live or travel abroad." Obviously, peregrinate is cognate with the adjective peregrine (which the RH2 defines as "foreign, alien, coming from abroad; wandering, traveling, or migrating"), and peregrine's etymology further illuminates the etymology of peregrinate. Peregrine is derived from the Latin *peregrinus*, "foreign," through *peregré*, which literally means "through the field" from the prefix *per-*, "through," the combining form (of *ager*) -*egr*-, "field," and the suffix -*é*, -ine.

❧ RARITY

Very rare

❧ WHY I LIKE THE WORD PEREGRINATE

The W3's "the air of one who has traveled or lived abroad" sold me on this word. What is that "air"? What was it 400 years ago? What is it today?

Of course, foreignness has always been fairly easy to discern. The combination of clothes, footwear and other accoutrements, hairstyle, skin tone and texture, mannerisms, and even gait usually offers enough visual clues to allow one not only to successfully pick out a tourist, but to have a darn good chance of picking their nationality, too.

But discerning peregrinity, or "worldliness"—now that's usually a much harder task. The same clues apply, but their presence will be watered down with local attire. So how do you know if those Moroccan sandals were bought in Casablanca or down the road at the local shoe importer's? You don't. You have to discern that "air." Does the person look as if he or she has seen the world? And has it left any mark on them, their accoutrements, their style, their mannerisms or, if all else fails, their accent?

❧ PEREGRINATE ALIVE

By rights, Jane should have been excited to finally meet the **peregrinate** writer standing before her, but all the meeting did was remind her of the long weekend she wished had never ended. The writer himself reminded her of Angelo, whom she wished she had never met.

perendinate

{pə-REN-də-neyt. Verb.}

ᴄᴏ MEANING

To perendinate means "to defer until the day after tomorrow; to postpone for a day." There is also an intransitive form that, historically, has meant "to stay at a university college, especially for an extended period of time" (OED Draft Revision Dec. 2005).

Perendinate differs only slightly from its synonym, procrastinate, through the timing of the postponement. While both *can* loosely be applied to any time in the future, more accurate usage has perendinating delaying the action until "the day after tomorrow," whereas procrastinating only delays the action until tomorrow.

The adjective is **perendinated**.

ᴄᴏ AGE

Mid-17th century

ᴄᴏ ETYMOLOGY

From the Latin *perendinat-*, from *perendinare*, "to defer until the day after tomorrow, to postpone for a day," from *perendinus*, "after tomorrow."[83] Perendinate's synonym, procrastinate, is derived from the Latin *procrastinatus*, from *procrastinare*, "to put off till the next day," from the prefix *pro-*, pro-, and *crastinus*, "belonging to tomorrow."[84]

ᴄᴏ RARITY

Extremely rare

ᴄᴏ WHY I LIKE THE WORD PERENDINATE

This is a very welcome addition to my lexical **armamentarium**. I can't wait to have an opportunity to look someone in the eye and confidently tell them that, yes, I shall perendinate whatever unimportant thing it is that they need "yesterday." With the right tone and non-verbals, it will come across precisely like, yes, I'm on to it. And, in 48 hours, I will be!

Oh yes, procrastinate is so "last year" now. I think we are all far too busy

Perhaps it was merely that people were far too engaged in ompha-loskepsis to be able to post to this thread so they **perendinated**.

pave_spectre, "Nothing to Say,"
PCGuide.com (discussion forum), 12 Sep. 2003[85]

to put things off for only a day. And even with its common meaning of an indefinite delay, it just sounds so stale and blunt when you compare it with perendinate.

And how about these three obsolete alternatives: nudiustertian, instead of "the day before yesterday"; pridian, instead of "yesterday"; and lustrum, instead of "a period of five years"?

Lastly, a note about the quotation. As with many of the extremely rare words in this book, finding a quote for perendinate was—and I need to pick just the right word here—challenging. The context in this case is a thread from what looks like a fairly standard computer forum. What is unusual is that this thread is not about computers, it's not about anything. And it's hundreds of postings and nearly 18 months of nothing. (By the way, *omphaloskepsis* is a fancy word for "navel gazing.")

⸞ PERENDINATE ALIVE

Jane's client, the famous author L. T. F. G. Dalziel, had not had time to sit down before Jane's infamous assistant signaled to her that Rosamund was on the phone.

"You know what, Mr Dalziel, we love your place, we love your project, and I will **perendinate** it forthwith."

L. T. F. G. (whatever that stood for) was lost for words—not a predicament to which he was accustomed. Jane pushed on, "So I will meet you at your place on Thursday—my assistant will arrange a time. It's so nice to see you. Good day."

Finally, a word escaped the writer's unusually full lips. "Splendid," he said with a smile.

peripeteia

{peh-rə-pə-TAI-ə or peh-rə-pə-TEE-ə. Noun.}

ᗢ MEANING

The OED (Draft Revision Dec. 2005) thus defines a peripeteia: "In classical tragedy (and hence in other forms of drama, fiction, etc.): a point in the plot at which a sudden reversal occurs. In extended use: a sudden or dramatic change; a crisis."

Significantly, the W3 also notes that such a reversal can also take place "in actual affairs."

ᗢ AGE

Late 16th century

ᗢ ETYMOLOGY

From the Latin *peripetia* "a turn right about, a sudden change," from the Greek *peripeteia*, from *peri-*, "around, about," and *piptein*, "to fall."

ᗢ RARITY

Rare

ᗢ WHY I LIKE THE WORD PERIPETEIA

Thankfully, I have written about many more peripeteias than I have experienced.

The key ingredients of a peripeteia are surprise, drama and suddenness. I suspect that, for most people, almost everything significant in life is a surprise—it has certainly been so for me. There have been plenty of plans and achievements, but the achievements have borne little resemblance to the original goals, the costs (mainly time) have always been higher than assumed, and the diversions and side-trips have been high in number and rich in reward.

So, most of the "actual" changes in my life have been persistently unexpected, but neither sudden nor dramatic, and I am grateful for this. I know that peripeteias do occur in real life and they do cause people to fall or, more accurately, to be knocked down.

In the fictional realm, my preference for peripeteias are those that lend themselves to my favorite plot type—the testing plot. These plots involve the protagonist slowly fighting his or her way back from several peripeteias of the magnitude that would knock down most of us for good. But the protagonist somehow absorbs the pain of all setbacks and, each time, gets back up, gets back on track, and moves one step closer to reward or redemption.

ᕙ PERIPETEIA ALIVE

Bill needed to find a way to convince Jerry that his "Paris episode" would not result in the kind of vocational **peripeteia** that Jerry had nightmares about: demotion. Jerry might just be able to cope with being fired, but being demoted was against the laws of his universe. Also on Bill's mind were the incessant musings he was having about a vocational peripeteia of his own: change. He suspected he had already passed the emotional point of no return and that it was only a matter of time before his thoughts manifested into actions, actions that he would have some difficulty explaining, especially to Jane. But Jerry would probably be thrilled.

perlustrate

{per-LUS-treyt. Verb.}

⌘ MEANING

As defined by the OED (Draft Revision Dec. 2005), to perlustrate is to perform one of two distinct actions:

1. To travel through and inspect thoroughly; to survey comprehensively, especially in an official capacity.
2. To examine a document for the purpose of surveillance; to intercept and read correspondence passing through the post.

The noun is **perlustration**. A **perlustrator** is "a person who examines or inspects thoroughly" (OED, Draft Revision Dec. 2007).

⌘ AGE
Mid-16th century

⌘ ETYMOLOGY
From the Latin *perlustrat-*, from *perlustrare*, "to travel through, to scrutinize," from the prefix *per-*, "through," and *lustrare*, "to traverse, survey, lustrate, brighten."

⌘ RARITY
Extremely rare

⌘ WHY I LIKE THE WORD PERLUSTRATE

At last I have found a verb to distinguish "doing" countries (*yeah, we did Italy, France, Spain, and then we flew to Cairo and did Egypt, too*) from the kind of traveling that turns my wheels: slow travel. And I have found another noun (after **omnist**) that fits me: I am a perlustrator.

Except for those few, unavoidable times when I am either very tired or much in need of a shower, I really do love to travel. I don't know which came first, wanderlust or the big philosophical questions, but either way an anthropologically slanted perlustration has worked well for me. Through observing people from different parts of the world I have been able to distinguish for myself behavior that is specific to culture, religion, climate and so on from behavior that is universal.

And how much perlustrating have I actually done? Well, because I am a perlustrator *and* a writer, I inspect thoroughly *and* keep notes. I can, therefore, tell you that since leaving school 22 years ago, I have been to 33 countries and slept in 424 different beds. In the first 10 years—which was, significantly I think, *before* I had an e-mail account—I visited 27 of those countries (82%) and slept in 300 of those beds (71%). If we take my native country out of both tallies, that gives me a ratio of 9 beds per foreign country: that's taking your time, that's perlustrating.

Depressingly, the figures after that time are too low to report and, while I concede that being a father for the past six years has certainly placed some limitations on slow travel, I am resolute that the chief cause of my dearth of travel is simply that my life is too busy, and the 24-7 accessibility and limitless nature of e-mail and the Internet plays a big role in that. Too many options! So I have been steadily regaining control, divesting myself of e-mail addresses, web businesses and anything that requires me to "log in."

❧ PERLUSTRATE ALIVE

So, thought Bill, if he did change direction, what would he do? Could he move to the country and open an antique store? He loved to **perlustrate** historical documents nearly as much as he loved to perlustrate countries. What he didn't want to do was to spend the rest of his life growing deeper into the lifestyle of his job, and growing further from the lifestyle of his interests and sensibilities.

petrichor

{PEH-trə-kor. Noun.}

MEANING

From the OED (Draft Revision Dec. 2005): "A pleasant, distinctive smell frequently accompanying the first rain after a long period of warm, dry weather in certain regions. Also: an oily liquid mixture of organic compounds which collects in the ground and is believed to be responsible for this smell."

Wikipedia, reporting on the *Nature* article quoted opposite, notes that "the smell derives from an oil exuded by certain plants during dry periods, whereupon it is adsorbed by clay-based soils and rocks. During rain, the oil is released into the air along with another compound, geosmin, producing the distinctive scent."[86] Note that "adsorbed" isn't a misspelling. Adsorption differs from absorption in that instead of a liquid or gas being soaked up, it "accumulates on the surface of a solid or a liquid (adsorbant), forming a molecular or atomic film (the adsorbate)."[87]

AGE

Mid-20th century

ETYMOLOGY

Petrichor is a recently coined geological term (see the quotation). It is derived from the Latin combining form *petr-*, from the Greek *petros*, "stone," or *petra*, "rock," and the Greek *ichor*, "the ethereal fluid supposed to flow like blood in the veins of the gods."[88]

RARITY

Very rare

WHY I LIKE THE WORD PETRICHOR

I *know* this wonderful, rejuvenating smell, but I had no idea it had a name—and what an interesting and well-chosen name it is—a euonym (literally, "good name") if ever there was one.

While our sense of smell is rudimentary compared with that of many animals, distinguishing more than just "nice" smells from "stinky" smells is well within our capability—if only we had a matching olfactory vocabulary.

Those who smell for a living, such as perfumers, develop terrifically
descriptive olfactory vocabularies. They are also aided by a framework of
olfactive families (such as floral, green, aldehydic, *Chypre*, woody, oriental,
citrus, and *Fougère*), a fragrance wheel (much like the color wheel), and
fragrance "notes" (top, middle and base notes for short-, medium- and longlasting fragrances, respectively). Alas, the rest of us are usually left lost for
words, and that is why I chose petrichor. Now, at least, there is one more smell
that we will all be able to name.

⌒ PETRICHOR ALIVE

Since his team's triumph at the fun run last month, Bill had been running more
than he usually did, and he knew exactly why. It wasn't just that he was carried
away by the win; his logical mind had simply told him that running more was
worth the effort, however you diced it. He had enjoyed the thrill of the win
and knew he would enjoy even more being one of the five runners whose times
were counted. He also knew that any improvement would only be better for
him and that it would also serve to spur on his teammates to run even faster.
And today, he enjoyed the additional payback of being unexpectedly rained
on, always pleasant when you are hot from exertion, but with the added bonus
of evoking that wonderful **petrichor** that always took his mind back to exotic
places and the happiest of memories.

philtrum

{FIL-trəm. Noun.}

MEANING
The W3 defines philtrum as "the vertical groove on the median line of the upper lip." The OED (Draft Entry Mar. 2006) clarifies the extent of the groove, which is "between the base of the nose and the border of the upper lip."

The OED also notes that philtrum is another word for philtre or philter, "a love potion."

The plural noun is **philtra**.

AGE
Early 17th century

ETYMOLOGY
From the Greek *philtron*, "love-charm, love-potion," from the combining form *phil-*, "to love," and the suffix *-tron*, which forms nouns of instruments, via Latin.

RARITY
Rare

WHY I LIKE THE WORD PHILTRUM
Of the words I *should* know, my anatomical vocabulary is not quite my worst, but nearly. That ignominy goes to my botanical vocabulary, which is limited to grass, weeds, shrubs, bushes, gorse, the names of about five flowers, and a similar number of trees and, as of very recently, a number of terms relating to legumes (see **papilionaceous**). I suspect the constant presence of my own body has helped to expand my anatomical vocabulary into perhaps the twenties, but it is still embarrassingly limited.

So I needed to choose at least one anatomical term, for my own benefit as well as the book's coverage.

The good news is, of course, that I discovered philtrum. According to Wikipedia, this seemingly insignificant physical feature "allows humans to express a much larger range of lip motions than would otherwise be possible, which enhances vocal and non-verbal communication."[89] So the usefulness of this "love instrument" goes beyond the erogenous qualities that clearly captivated the Greeks.

As you can imagine, in my "travels" through the dictionaries and other sources, I stumbled upon numerous anatomical terms and several were vying for inclusion. Of the runners-up, I just want to mention one, the intertragic notch. It refers to the notch at the base of the inside of your ear (directly above your earlobe) where you slot those little headphones if your intertragic notch is deep enough, which mine is. However, my wife's intertragic notch is wide and shallow, which means in-ear headphones won't stay lodged and she has to wear bulkier, less fashionable over-ear headphones, which of course annoys her and is basically the end of the world.

And if you want to know what the little flaps at the top of the intertragic notch are called (and, yes, I am really just posing this rhetorical question so I can show off), the anterior one (the one closest to your face) is called the tragus, and the posterior one, not surprisingly, is called the antitragus.

❧ PHILTRUM ALIVE

As Jane was being escorted by Dalziel on a tour of his apartment, she was disconcerted by her own uncontrollable urge to keep looking at him rather than at his simple surroundings. His mesmerizing face was Clooneyesque on top—short dark hair, piercing brown eyes—and Travoltaesque below, complete with pronounced **philtrum** and matching dimple. Mmm, yes, she could look at that face all day.

phrontistery

{FROHN-tis-ter-ee. Noun; also **phrontisterion**.}

↬ MEANING
The W3 succinctly defines a phrontistery as "a place for thinking or study."

↬ AGE
Early 17th century

↬ ETYMOLOGY
From the Greek *phrontistërion*, a "thinking-shop" (apparently coined by the Greek playwright Aristophanes to ridicule the school of his contemporary, Socrates),[90] from *phrontistës*, "phrontist, deep thinker," and the noun-forming suffix *-tërion*, via Latin.

↬ RARITY
Very rare

↬ WHY I LIKE THE WORD PHRONTISTERY
If you have heard of "the person from Porlock" you will know where I am going to go with this word: interruptions. Where can we go these days to escape them?

The person from Porlock is a literary allusion to an unwanted intruder, particularly where the person being interrupted is an artist in the middle of his or her creative process. The allusion stems from an unverified story by Samuel Taylor Coleridge that he was interrupted by a person from Porlock while he was in the middle of writing an inspirational poem, which he was then unable to complete properly.

In today's world of electronic communication, I often feel like there is an entire army of Porlockians camped outside my house, each patiently waiting his turn to interrupt me at precisely the wrong moment. I hide in my office at the rear of the house, ignore the landline, switch off the mobile, and shut down my e-mail program . . . and then someone's house alarm goes off!

I do have a private place to think (the shower) but not write, and I have makeshift phrontisteries at a dozen cafés and libraries. But I do not, at present, have a phrontistery that is mine or that I can rely on. When I was a child, my bedroom was my phrontistery. Don't parents today realize that as soon as they "reward" their children with the old family television (after the obligatory upgrade to a massive new power-hungry LCD or plasma television), the chances are that the phrontistery will vanish in the noisy glare of the cathode-ray tube?

⚬ PHRONTISTERY ALIVE

Dalziel fixed Jane with his George Clooney eyes. It was time to get down to the essence of the matter. "What I need, Jane, is a **phrontistery**. Do you understand?"

Jane nodded, "Yes, my husband shares your desire."

This innocent but somewhat ambiguous statement caused Dalziel, a man highly skilled at the art of the double entendre, to break off his gaze and shift in his chair. Jane blushed and wondered if all their conversations were going to be this intense. She certainly hoped so.

plesiosynchronous

{plee-zee-oh-SIN(G)-krə-nəs. Adjective; also **plesiochronous**.}

◌ MEANING

Plesiosynchronous means "nearly simultaneous" and is a variant of the more common plesiochronous, which the OED (Draft Entry Sept. 2006) defines as "designating or relating to systems which are operating with clocks that are not perfectly synchronized with each other."

The noun is (presumably) **plesiosynchronicity**.

◌ AGE

Late 20th century

◌ ETYMOLOGY

From the Greek combining forms *plesio-*, "near," *syn-*, "alike," and *-chronos*, "a period of time." Exactly who coined the term is unclear. The OED's first citation is from an international electronics congress held in Rome, Italy, in 1974.

◌ RARITY

Extremely rare

◌ WHY I LIKE THE WORD PLESIOSYNCHRONOUS

This is a handy word, usefully filling the lexical gap between simultaneous and "almost at the same time," which could refer to a lag of a millisecond or a year, depending on the context. Plesiosynchronous specifically means the former—a fraction of a second—and has special uses in the telecommunications industry. But the rest of us can use this word to describe the many situations in life when cause and effect are plesiosynchronous. But before providing some examples of this, I should explain why I chose "plesiosynchronous" instead of the original and more common "plesiochronous": it makes more sense and it sounds better. And clearly I am not the only one who thinks this, otherwise the variant wouldn't exist.

Now to the fun stuff: things in everyday life that are plesiosynchronous. The first thing that came to mind for me was the plesiosynchronicity in our house of the opening of a box of a particular brand of chocolates and the consumption of the first chocolate by my chocoholic wife. A more common (perhaps, perhaps not?) example would be the response of a parent to a child in danger or distress (I swear we used to wake up a millisecond *before* our girls cried out at night when they were newborns). An example from the world of sports is when, for example, your beloved West Ham is 1–3 down to Manchester United with seven minutes to go and you are just hanging in there, hoping for a goal that could give you a sniff of an equalizer and a well-earned point away and then Man U scores, it's 1–4, and you and 15,000 other West Ham supporters are already on your feet and heading for the coaches. And, of course, the reaction times of top sportspeople are all plesiosynchronous with whatever they are reacting to.

I guess U2 concert tickets going on sale and being sold out are *not* plesiosynchronous events, but it sure seems like it.

∽ PLESIOSYNCHRONOUS ALIVE

Jane seldom boasted about it but, more often than not, seeing a room for the first time and having a pretty good idea of how to bring out the best in that room were, for her, **plesiosynchronous** events. Her instinctive talent had been honed by years of study and hard work, but it was still instinctive and, right now, it was telling her to leave the writer's apartment alone.

Despite his pretentious name and (according to some) books, he was one of the least pretentious people she had ever met. And his apartment was the same. It was distinctive, peaceful and personal. Why would he, or she, want to change that?

plutomania

{ploo-toh-MEYN-ee-ə. Noun.}

ᴥ MEANING

Plutomania doesn't appear in the RH2, but the OED (Draft Revision Sept. 2006) and W3 have congruous entries, each listing two definitions: "excessive or frenzied pursuit of wealth" (OED), "excessive or abnormal desire for wealth" (W3); "a delusional belief that one possesses immense wealth" (OED), "insanity marked by delusions of wealth" (W3).

The adjective is **plutomanic**.

ᴥ AGE

Mid-17th century

ᴥ ETYMOLOGY

From the Greek combining form *plouto-*, "wealth, riches," and the Latin *mania*, "excessive desire, mental illness."

ᴥ RARITY

Extremely rare

ᴥ WHY I LIKE THE WORD PLUTOMANIA

One of the OED's citations for this word states that "plutomania is absolutely pandemic."[92] That quote is from 1953. Crikey, if it was pandemic then, what is it now?

We Westerners may not all be plutomaniacs, but we sure act as if we are. Is our desire for wealth not "excessive"? Do we even know what *isn't* excessive, that is, what we actually need? Are our lives, which revolve around the "pursuit of wealth," not "frenzied"? Are our governments not increasingly plutocratic? If it looks like a duck and it walks like a duck . . .

I am pleased that there is a word for this "abnormal desire" and that my generalization directly above (in which the abnormal is normal) is just that, a generalization. There is a growing section of society that can clearly see the demarcation between useful and superfluous; between need, want and waste. These people are down-sizing, simplifying; they are not opting out, they are just opting—making choices—and with each promotion and demotion, that which is left becomes more valued and, therefore, more valuable. Let me put it another way. If you only have five favorite possessions, are you likely to value, use, enjoy and care for them more than if they are merely your five favorite possessions among 100 that you mildly desire? It is surely not possible to enjoy those five possessions as much in the second scenario, because the other 95 consume resources (money to buy and maintain them, time to use them, space to store them).

So if you have plutomania or, perhaps worse still, oniomania ("the compulsive urge to buy things; an uncontrollable desire for acquisition"[94]), then be wary; possessions cost significantly more than just their purchase price.

It seems acutely ironic to me that, at this time of unprecedented plutomania, the verb "to pluto" has been coined in response to the declassification of the (former) planet: "to demote or devalue someone or something."[95] The way I see it, we need to pluto our desire for wealth and turbocharge our desire for value.

❧ PLUTOMANIA ALIVE

Bill was used to a status quo in the Mitchell household in which Jane did the **plutomania**, partly for the success it signified, but mainly for the shopping it supported. But Bill's recurring dream of a new life (and perhaps a country estate) meant that, for the first time in his life, he was fueled by the fire of financial ambition.

pluviose

{PLOO-vee-ohs or PLOO-vee-ohz. Adjective; also **pluvious**.}

ᖚ MEANING

The OED (Draft Revision Sept. 2006) defines pluviose (the **adjective**) as: "Of, relating to, or characterized by rain; rainy."

There is also a proper noun, ***Pluviôse***, which is the only form the RH2 lists. It thus defines the word: "(in the French Revolutionary calendar) the fifth month of the year, extending from January 20 to February 18." According to the OED and Wikipedia, this isn't totally accurate as the 30-day-long month sometimes began on January 19 or 20, depending on the year. Clearly that time of year is rainy in France, hence the name. And, yes, the month starting in July was named "hot" (*Fervidor*), the one starting in December was named "snow" (*Nivôse*), and the one starting in February was named "wind" (*Ventôse*). The calendar certainly made a lot of sense but suffered greatly from the tiny issue of there being 365 or 366 days in a year, not 360. First used in 1793, the calendar only lasted for about 13 years.

The noun is **pluviosity**.

ᖚ AGE

Early 19th century

ᖚ ETYMOLOGY

From the Latin *pluviosus*, "rainy."

ᖚ RARITY

Very rare

ᖚ WHY I LIKE THE WORD PLUVIOSE

Okay, we already have the adjective rainy, so why have I chosen this word, other than for the curious etymology of its cognate, *Pluviôse?*

I admit this is at best tenuous, but the OED's citations included a figurative use of pluviose (as "tearful") in an 1824 quote—"I was moved to vent my pluviose indignation"[96]—and this just tickled my fancy. I haven't been able to find a single other quotation of the word used figuratively, but I don't care,

I think "pluviose indignation" works. It certainly sounds like a superlative version of tearful indignation, and rainy indignation certainly doesn't work—and neither does rainy tears or, worse still, tears raining down. But pluviose tears works for me (big, freely flowing tears), possibly pluviose eyes, certainly a pluviose leak or a steady, pluviose drip.

Yes, I think pluviose is well suited to figurative and poetic use: it sounds poetic, it's physical, it's visual, and it has plenty of historic connotations. But if it doesn't work for you in this way, you can at least use it (à la **perendinate** and procrastinate) as a substitute for rainy so that you can unreservedly whine about the weather without depressing everyone around you.

✎ PLUVIOSE ALIVE

"It's him again," thought Jane, as she glimpsed an unfamiliar yet familiar profile through the frosted glass at the front of her office. Why had he come? He didn't have an appointment. Surely he wouldn't just turn up. What if he *wasn't* coming to see her? Or was he checking up on her—on progress (of which there hadn't been any)?

Then, a knock, and the George/John face peered in. "Sorry to disturb, just saying hello. Left my umbrella here the other day and one can't really do without it in such a **pluviose** city. Anyway, I hope it's going well. If you have any questions, just call me. Must dash."

And he did.

poshlost

{PUSH-lost. Noun; also **pushlust**.}

◈ MEANING

Michael A. Fischer's prolific *worthless word for the day* web site defines poshlost as "a well-rounded, untranslatable whole made up of banality, vulgarity and sham; it applies not only to obvious trash (verbal and animate), but also to spurious beauty, spurious importance, spurious cleverness."[97] I have seen the same definition attributed to Russian-American novelist Vladimir Nabokov and, though it sounds as though it might have been coined by Nabokov (based on confirmed quotations) I cannot confirm whether it was.

While poshlost does not yet appear in my dictionaries, there is a detailed article on the term in Wikipedia.[98] The article provides no fewer than five definitions, including this (confirmed) one from Nabokov: "[poshlost] is not only the obviously trashy but mainly the falsely important, the falsely beautiful, the falsely clever, the falsely attractive."[99]

The other definitions—all from books about Nabokov in particular or Russian literature in general—include Vladimir Alexandrov's pithy "petty evil or self-satisfied vulgarity"[100] and Svetlana Boym's intriguing summary: "Poshlost is the Russian version of banality, with a characteristic national flavoring of metaphysics and high morality, and a peculiar conjunction of the sexual and the spiritual. This one word encompasses triviality, vulgarity, sexual promiscuity, and a lack of spirituality. The war against poshlost is a cultural obsession of the Russian and Soviet intelligentsia from the 1860s to 1960s."[101]

◈ AGE

Early 20th century

◈ ETYMOLOGY

Poshlost is a loanword from Russian. IMDB.com (the Internet Movie Database) lists *Ostorozhno: poshlost* as a 1959 Russian film directed by Elem Klimov. The English translation: *Attention: Vulgarity*!

◈ RARITY

Extremely rare

∾ WHY I LIKE THE WORD POSHLOST

I have chosen this word precisely because it makes me think. It partly makes sense to me, but whether you "get it" or not, its meaning is far from concrete. I don't know exactly what I would describe as poshlost (though someone I know suggested *King Kong*, shopping malls, Disneyland and MTV).[102] Poshlost poses helpful questions: it is **maieutic**. Is much of our daily news poshlost? Vulgar sound-bites of spurious importance? I suspect so.

∾ POSHLOST ALIVE

"I mean, I think he's quite unusual, and I like that, and I don't want to change him or his apartment, which is . . . difficult." Jane didn't really know what she was saying to Bill but she needed to talk about her predicament with someone and it might as well be her husband. "You do know who he is, don't you?'

"Yes, yes," Bill nodded, "he writes **poshlost**—always throwing in crass generalizations and banal vulgarities. Quite good fun, really. So what are you going to do?"

presque vu

{pres-keh-VOO. Noun.}

❧ MEANING

Once again, Wikipedia steps up to the plate: "the sensation of being on the brink of an epiphany. Often very disorienting and distracting, presque vu rarely leads to an actual breakthrough. Frequently, one experiencing presque vu will say that they have something 'on the tip of their tongue.'"[103]

❧ AGE

Mid-20th century

❧ ETYMOLOGY

Presque vu is a borrowing from French. Closely related to déjà vu ("already seen"), it consists of the adverb *presque*, "already, near," and the past participle *vu*, "that which is seen," from the verb *voir*, "to see."

❧ RARITY

Very rare

❧ WHY I LIKE THE PHRASE PRESQUE VU

It is certainly a fact of my life that I often feel like I have come agonizingly close to seeing, remembering, grasping or deducing something important only to have the thought process stall prior to delivery. Sometimes it is the answer to a question that has failed to arrive, but just as often it is the conclusion to a statement that I foolishly began without knowing exactly how it was going to end.

While we should all be grateful for the existence of the closely related phrase, "tip of the tongue," presque vu offers legitimacy for a different level of cognitive failure. Typically, it is a name or some other item of trivia that has only made it as far as the tip of your tongue, but the things that we have "nearly seen" are anything but trivial—they are epiphanies, breakthroughs, big stuff.

And given that my friends and family know only too well that I regularly contemplate the big questions of life, I am hopeful that presque vu will go some way towards exonerating me on the many occasions when all that thinking doesn't quite produce, well, anything.

I guess presque vu could be seen as the flipside to **afterwit**. If the synchronicity of seeing and needing to see is the goal—that is, gainfully employed knowledge—then presque vu is not seeing, and afterwit is seeing too late. In any case, I expect I will gain more mileage out of presque vu than I ever have out of déjà vu.

∾ PRESQUE VU ALIVE

Rain! Jane had just been mentally revisiting Dalziel's umbrella visit and . . . something! There was something in the whole pluviose-city-any-questions thing. A clue! Maybe a clue. But she had seen something. What? It really was bad timing for **presque vu**, she thought, getting more and more frustrated. What she needed was just plain old *vu*, and she needed it chop-chop.

proficuous

{prə-FIK-yoo-əs. Adjective.}

☙ MEANING

The OED (Draft Revision Dec. 2007) defines proficuous as "profitable; beneficial, useful." The W3 defines it a full one-third more concisely as merely "profitable, useful," but the OED gets my vote (for reasons explained below).

Interestingly, the W3 also designates proficuous as "obsolete." I am pleased to report that my research supports the OED's position that this is not the case.

☙ AGE

Early 17th century

☙ ETYMOLOGY

From the Latin *proficuus*, "profitable, advantageous, beneficial, useful" from *proficere*, "to make progress, to profit" and the adjective-forming suffix, *-uus*, -ous.

☙ RARITY

Extremely rare

☙ WHY I LIKE THE WORD PROFICUOUS

The combination of profitable *and* useful *and* beneficial in the same concept is, I think, a hugely valuable one.

I believe that our economic system (which, sadly, is the cornerstone of our culture), based as it is on the twin assumptions of perpetual growth and the innate benefit of all economic activity, is flawed. Morever, within a finitely resourced biosphere, it is illogical, unethical, short-sighted, and just plain dippy. So words like proficuous and **plutomania** cannot be revived quickly enough for me. We need to discuss the merits, limitations, effects, and appropriateness of the beast of economic activity that controls not only the quality of our lives, but the quality of the biosphere itself.

I think all economic activity needs to be and should be proficuous, in the widest possible sense. The trader can certainly hang on to the profits, but the

ᴑ QUOTATION ᴑ

Indipendent [sic] of any scholastic ties, Haydn and Tomasini were united by a mutual esteem and admiration which resulted in a longlasting and **proficuous** collaboration.

"TC.742001—Luigi Tomasini—Trios for two violins and cello,"
Tactus, May 2003[104]

trader's product or service should be useful, not just to the trader (solely for the purpose of generating those profits), but also to the consumer. And the overall effect of the economic activity, for the full life cycle of the product or service, should produce a net benefit to society at large. And surely every single person in business should be a social entrepreneur, because all business is ultimately dependent upon a strong and healthy society. And surely every single person in business should be a green entrepreneur, because a strong and healthy society is ultimately dependent upon a healthy and well-resourced environment.

I had hoped I would find examples of this word used in business language, but it is alive and well only in academia, where you will find proficuous applications, collaborations, co-operations, exchanges, discussions and interactions. But I know the word has currency in a business environment because in the last few months since learning the word, I have already had at least half a dozen occasions to use it, and I have grasped every one.

ᴑ PROFICUOUS ALIVE

Bill and Jerry's change-management program was waning. No one *really* got it, and Bill was starting to wonder if even the ever-compliant Jerry truly understood the principles behind what they were trying to change. To Bill, it was painfully obvious: If the result of a manager's activity was not **proficuous**, then that manager should be doing something differently, or doing a different job. So much of people's busyness was counter-productive or futile, but everyone was so wedded to the merry-go-round that they couldn't see it. You needed to get off it, take several steps back, and then look at it, which is what Bill knew he had to do with his whole life.

quaquaversal

{kway-kwə-VER-səl. Adjective.}

◈ MEANING

The OED (Draft Revision Dec. 2007) categorises quaquaversal as a "chiefly geological" term and defines it as "dipping, pointing, or occurring in every direction."

The RH2 defines quaquaversal as "sloping downward from the center in all directions," qualified as "of a geological formation."

The noun is **quaquaversality**. The adverb is **quaquaversally**.

◈ AGE

Early 18th century

◈ ETYMOLOGY

From the Latin *quaqua versus*, "turned in every direction," from *quaqua*, "wherever, in whatever direction," and *versus*, from *vertere*, "to turn."

◈ RARITY

Very rare

◈ WHY I LIKE THE WORD QUAQUAVERSAL

Imagine this scene. From a bird's-eye view you can see a large and busy picnic taking place in a very large park. In the picnic group are 10–12 adults and 16 toddlers. Now imagine, if you will, the 16 toddlers running off, quaquaversally, and the slightly outnumbered parents frantically chasing after them.

This image is a very real one for me and it is what instantly came to mind when I discovered the word quaquaversal. You see, my wife and I attended multiple-birth prenatal classes so we became friends with the parents of eight other sets of twins. After the births, all but one of the families stayed in close contact, so events like the one described above were common. And, due to the dads working (that is, having jobs outside the home), there were always fewer parents than children.

So how do you chase two children who are heading in different directions? (You just grab one and yell very loudly and compellingly at the other.)

My next engagement with quaquaversal was just a couple of months
ago when I was speaking to an osteopath who was telling me how some of
our muscles "turn in every direction." Of course, I piped up with my new
word which I think impressed him. As quaquaversal is a geological term it is
no wonder he hadn't come across it in *Gray's Anatomy*, but we agreed it still
worked.

And my most recent interaction with the word was when I was searching
for quotations and found the delightful one above, which immediately made
me think of the guaranteed quaquaversal state of my hair when I wake up in
the morning. I tell you, this word needs to be set free from the confines of
"geological formation." We need it up here on *terra firma*.

⟶ QUAQUAVERSAL ALIVE

Bill knew he had plenty of options, but usually options were grouped into
a couple of streams that you could trade off against each other to uncover
your über-option. But this time his options seemed to be **quaquaversal**,
each taking him in a distinct direction. He could dig in deeper at work, just
pushing harder until he effected the changes he knew were so needed; he could
continue to juggle his private and professional lives and genuinely make the
best of his circumstances; or he could actively change direction and become a
new, reconciled Bill, doing new stuff.

reify

{REE-ə-fai or RAY-ə-fai. Verb.}

MEANING

According to the W3, to reify is "to regard (an abstraction, a mental construction) as a thing: convert mentally into something concrete or objective: give definite content and form to: materialize." The dictionary illustrates its definition with two quotes, including: "a culture can be reified into a body of traditions— M. J. Herskovits."

The RH2 notes that you can also "reify a concept."

The noun is **reification**.

AGE

Mid-19th century

ETYMOLOGY

From the Latin *res*, "a thing," and the verb-forming suffix -ify.

RARITY

Rare

WHY I LIKE THE WORD REIFY

If a culture can be reified into a body of traditions, an education can be reified into the fruits of a teacher's labors. And a parent's attentiveness can be reified into the achievements of a secure child. And an inventor's concept can be reified into a working device. And an artist's vision can be reified into a painting. And a writer's ideas can be reified into a book. Oh, yeah, I like this word.

I am fascinated by human motivations. *Why* do we do the things we do? Are our needs and motivations substantively the same; the manner in which we satisfy them the source of our diversity? Only if you can motivate can you educate, and only if you educate can you learn from the past and hope to succeed in the future. My experience tells me that if you can reify concepts you are much more likely to engage students and successfully transform words on a page into useful, motivating knowledge.

⟡ REIFY ALIVE

Meanwhile, Jane has had an epiphany—her designer's block blown away by
the crucial realization that she had been thinking about everything inside out.
Dalziel wanted a phrontistery and she would give him one by transforming
his attic into a small office and rooftop garden, and she would leave the rest of
the interior alone. What triggered the epiphany was the realization that if his
book- and art-laden apartment wasn't already a phrontistery then something
new had to be introduced. And that thing was nature—the nature that steered
all life, but from an increasing distance. Jane just had to reduce that distance.
All she needed was the right architect and builder, and she knew that, together,
they could and would **reify** her vision into exactly what L. T. F. G. Dalziel
needed.

rusticate

{RUS-tə-keyt. Verb.}

❧ MEANING

Rusticate is a polysemic verb with six standard definitions. Here is the RH2's entry (note, the first two are for "rusticate" as an intransitive verb, the last four are for the word as a transitive verb):

1. to go to the country.
2. to stay or sojourn in the country.
3. to send to or domicile in the country.
4. to make rustic, as persons or manners.
5. to finish (a wall surface) so as to produce or suggest rustication.
6. *British* to suspend (a student) from a university as punishment.

The OED's and W3's entries are very similar, but I will just add a few choice words from the OED. For the first definition, "to retire to the country"; for the second, "to live a country life"; for the fourth, "to imbue with rural manners; to countrify"; for the sixth, "to 'send down.'"

The noun is **rustication**.

❧ AGE

Mid-17th century

❧ ETYMOLOGY

From the Latin *rusticatus*, from *rusticari*, "to live in the country," from *rusticus*, "rustic, countrified," from *rus*, "country," and -tic.

❧ RARITY

Very rare

❧ WHY I LIKE THE WORD RUSTICATE

At this particular time in my life, rusticate is much more than an interesting verb, it is a goal. I have done most of the downshifting I can do in a big, spread-out city, so now it is time to rusticate. But why? And to where?

As with all major decisions, one needs to begin with a picture of the goal. For us, the goal is to retain all of the great things about our current family life while addressing three key deficiencies.

First, "by a country mile," is the need to slow down. This has three key components: health (enough said), peace and quiet (enough said) and geographical detachment from the nature of city life.

The second driver is the need for more nature. We want at least some of our lives to pass in a location where we can be overwhelmed by the stars, be serenaded by the sounds of nature, and bear witness to the vibrant rhythms of nature's calendar.

The third driver is the need for a true adventure—something to which we really don't know how we will respond.

And to where will we rusticate? We haven't quite decided, but the Lake District (see the quotation) sure sounds good—the classic quiet life punctuated with "hot pursuits"!

⨀ RUSTICATE ALIVE

Bill decided it was time to involve Jane in his thoughts about a change of lifestyle. He knew she liked things put bluntly so he didn't bother dressing it up. "Jane, I've had an idea. Let's **rusticate**."

"What!"

"Move to the country."

"I know what it means, dear, but why on earth would we want to do that? Where would I shop?"

salariat

{sə-LEYR-ee-at. Noun.}

∾ MEANING

Here are the definitions, in full, from each of the three dictionaries.

OED: "The salaried class; salary-earners collectively."

RH2: "The class of workers in an economy who receive salaries."

W3: "The class or body of salaried persons usually as distinguished from wage earners."

I don't know if they try to phrase things differently on purpose or not, but it is interesting to note how many ways, in English at least, you can say the same thing.

∾ AGE

Early 20th century

∾ ETYMOLOGY

From the Latin *salarium*, "salary" (originally, the "money allowed to Roman soldiers for the purchase of salt, hence, their pay"),[106] after proletariat ("wage earners"), via French.

∾ RARITY

Very rare

∾ WHY I LIKE THE WORD SALARIAT

This may sound strange, but this word possesses an exotic quality for me. I will explain. My full-time working life has so far spanned 18 (stupidly busy) years, but I have been a salary earner for only 27 months of that time. I had my first "real" job in 1996. I was 28, and it (or should I say, I) lasted for nine months. My second (and last) salaried position lasted 18 months, ending in March 1999, nearly nine years ago.

Because I keep track of such things, I can tell you that during that same 18-year period I spent nearly 55 months overseas. So a salary (and sick days, holiday pay, office politics and office parties) are all, by the test of familiarity, twice as exotic to me as travel.

In fact, I have almost forgotten what being part of the salariat feels like. My memory is that it was simultaneously comfortable and uncomfortable: I enjoyed the benefits but, overall, it didn't feel right. So, as with **poshlost**, the idea of a salariat poses many questions. What effects does it have on society, given that (at its present size) it is still a relatively new phenomenon? Is it a good thing? I assume the stability it engenders produces many benefits, but I know that salaried positions typically involve a certain amount of excess and I don't know if that is truly affordable in the grand scheme of things. And what does being a lifelong member of the salariat mean to a human being? Obviously I will never know the answer to that question first-hand, but surely the overall tone and pattern of a person's life is affected by whether they are a wage earner, a salary earner, an employer, a beneficiary, a domestic worker (and by that I mean homemakers, not housemaids) or a supported person who chooses not to work.

As I said, the idea of a salariat poses many questions, but I cannot see any of the answers.

∽ SALARIAT ALIVE

Despite Jane's less-than-positive response, Bill couldn't stop questioning his position, not just geographically, but within the **salariat**. He needed change—they both did—and he would keep asking questions until, together, they found the right answers.

saudade

{SAH-u-dah-deh or (Brazilian Portuguese) SAH-u-dazh-ə. Noun.}

ᖰᕬ MEANING

The OED defines saudade as "longing, melancholy, nostalgia, as a supposed characteristic of the Portuguese or Brazilian temperament." This isn't a bad effort, but saudade is one of those words for which a body of citations will reveal more than a single, summarizing definition. The quotation, which is the OED's first citation, is particularly popular, and this immediately incited me to search for something "new." But, inevitably, I came back to it, presumably because of the same qualities that compelled the OED and all those other publications and writers to choose it. But another of the OED's citations is also worthy of re-citing. How about this gem from South African poet, Ignatius Roy Dunnachie Campbell: "that mysterious melancholy which sighs at the back of every joy" (*Portugal*, 1957).

Wikipedia's extensive article on saudade offers no direct translation, saying that "translation is dependent on context." It does offer a description—"a feeling of longing for something that one is fond of, which is gone, but might return in a distant future"[108]—but its very treatment of the word communicates that it is not a word that belongs in a box.

ᖰᕬ AGE
Early 20th century

ᖰᕬ ETYMOLOGY
Saudade is a loanword from Portuguese.

ᖰᕬ RARITY
Rare

ᖰᕬ WHY I LIKE THE WORD SAUDADE
I "get" this word (unlike **poshlost**). It's not melancholy, it's not nostalgia, it's not sadness, it's not wistfulness and it's not homesickness. Saudade is a mixture of the meanings of all of these words, spiced up with just a sprinkling of pride and joy.

A very long time ago I was melancholic over a lost love, and the melancholy was addictive: it showed I cared about her and about matters of the heart, and I didn't want to let it go. But, ultimately, it was a negative emotion—it produced nothing but weariness. Today I have saudade, not for her, but for some of the intoxicating feelings and experiences that I associate with her and with that period of my life. And, crucially, I still believe that experiences and feelings *akin* to that time are possible. Of course, so much of the equation would be different—better—but some valued elements that have been missing for a long time might return.

Saudade can also apply to a long-distance romance when each person is happy for the other person to be doing what they need to do and can draw pleasure from imagining them elsewhere, but are simultaneously knocked sideways that they are so far away and out of reach. A similar saudade applies to missing home and loved ones. I think New Zealand sports teams and supporters often experience saudade when they are overseas, particularly when they perform the haka. There is pride and joy in representing their country, mixed with a sadness for all those not able to be there.

⌒ SAUDADE ALIVE

Underlying Bill's motivation for change was a **saudade** he had for the days before management teams and multinationals, before personal organizers and personal trainers. He wanted to regain a certain quality that characterized those days, and that meant jumping ship. He wouldn't stop working, he would just work on something more immediate, more hands-on, more local. There is a word for that, he thought. And if he hadn't been so worn out from his ridiculously busy lifestyle he would probably have been able to remember it.

schlimmbesserung

{SHLIM-bes-er-ung. Noun.}

୶ MEANING

Remember the OOO *Drachenfutter* and Howard Rheingold's book, *They Have a Word for It?* Well I *think* this word (which also isn't in any of my dictionaries, any German-English dictionaries that I can lay my hands on, or in Wikipedia or Wiktionary) also first appeared in an English publication in Rheingold's book. I *think* because I haven't actually been able to track down a copy of his book to check it.

And just to add a little extra mystery, the references I found for *Drachenfutter* led me exclusively to a UK (Severn House) version of the book, whereas the references I have found for *Schlimmbesserung* lead exclusively to a US (Jeremy P. Tarcher) version. Both were published in 1988.[109]

In any case, reportedly, Rheingold defines *Schlimmbesserung* as "a so-called improvement that makes things worse."[110]

୶ AGE

Late 20th century

୶ ETYMOLOGY

As I have said above, my assumption is that Rheingold introduced this loanword from German to English readers in 1988. The word's components bear out its translation with *schlimm* being a German adjective meaning "bad," and *Besserung* being a German noun (from the adjective *besser*, "better") meaning "improvement." So the literal translation would be "bad improvement," a charming oxymoron if ever there was one.

୶ RARITY

Extremely rare

୶ WHY I LIKE THE WORD SCHLIMMBESSERUNG

Bad improvements are a part of life and this word needs to make a long overdue entrance into, at the very least, our children's vocabulary. Let me explain why.

Imagine you are seven years old and you have finally been allowed to use the scissors by yourself. Understandably carried away by the occasion, you unwisely decide to see how they work on your hair. Of course, you learn very quickly that they work just fine on your hair, but by now there is a divot of hair missing from your fringe. At this point, *if* you knew the word *Schlimmbesserung*, you would hold up your hand and solemnly tell your mother not to commit the *Schlimmbesserung* that the whole world knows her "fix-up trim" will become. But, alas, without the intervention of such an apt and sobering word the "improvement" ensues and, instead of your small and explicable nick, you are left with a devastatingly humiliating bowl-cut.

∾ SCHLIMMBESSERUNG ALIVE

Jane and the writer were standing in the middle of his fabulous new attic office, their backs to the rooftop garden that was still under construction on the other side of the wall of glass behind them.

"Hmm," muttered Dalziel, looking at the other three walls, "you've changed the color. What is it?"

Jane thought about this and, with uncharacteristic resignation (not to mention a commendably straight face), she answered, "*Schlimmbesserung.*"

"Oh?" Dalziel took a moment to properly consider the color, never thinking for a second to question an interior designer about its name. "Yes, it does have that sort of Teutonic look about it. Though I don't think I actually like it."

somnifugous

{sohm-NEE-f(y)u-jəs. Adjective.}

⚘ MEANING

The OED's entry for somnifugous simply quotes Nathan Bailey's *An Universal Etymological English Dictionary* (1721): "Driving away sleep."

The noun is **somnifuge**.

⚘ AGE

Early 18th century

⚘ ETYMOLOGY

Formed from the combining forms somni-, from the Latin *somnus*, sleep, and -fuge, "one that drives away" from the Latin *fugare*, "to put to flight." This latter component should be familiar (remember **dolorifuge**).

⚘ RARITY

Extremely rare

⚘ WHY I LIKE THE WORD SOMNIFUGOUS

Reading through one particular list of rare words, I stumbled upon somnifugous and, having already discovered **dolorifuge**, I immediately knew what it meant. I thought, this is another great word because there are so many things, particularly in modern-day life, that "drive away sleep," and I wondered why we don't call on such a perfectly constructed adjective to describe our **armamentarium** of sleep shunners.

And then, not many words later, I stumbled upon "soporiferous," which is an obsolete variant of soporific ("inducing or tending to induce sleep"), and it immediately reminded me of a joke by the brilliant, dry-witted comedian Steven Wright (the man who famously said, "It's a small world, but I wouldn't want to paint it"). Now, I won't try to tell you the joke "in my own words" because that would be inviting a ***Schlimmbesserung***. So I quote: "For my birthday I got a humidifier and a dehumidifier. I put them in the same room and let them fight it out."

It's like driving and coffee, or curtains and glowing alarm clocks.

So now that we have somnifugous to call upon, we won't have to talk about that thing that "prevented you from getting to sleep" or "disrupted your sleep," or "gave you a bad night's sleep," or "kept you awake," or "kept you up," or "kept you up half the night" and so on. You can just talk about that somnifugous worry, toothache, coffee, movie, neighbor's stereo, barking dog, flickering street light, or . . . carnal desire.

And the next time you are in need of a serious caffeine hit, why not ask your local barista for a somnifugous-strength coffee and see what happens!

❧ SOMNIFUGOUS ALIVE

Jane was waiting for Bill when he arrived home. She had champagne ready to pour and was wearing, for the first time, one of the dresses she'd bought with Bill on her last great shopping spree. Her next shopping spree, she had reason to believe, would almost certainly not be with Bill, and this was the reason for the celebration. "She's coming home, tomorrow."

Bill beamed from ear to ear. "That's great news."

"With Angelo, unfortunately, but it's another step in the right direction. Let's celebrate."

Bill had been dog-tired just a few seconds earlier, but the news of Rosamund's return and the sight of Jane in her gorgeous new dress were equally **somnifugous** and he was now wide awake and ready to celebrate.

sonsy

{SON-zee. Adjective; also **sonse**, **sonsie**.}

ᕱᕵ MEANING

As promised in the **kalon** entry, this is the Scottish word for a female who
is beautiful and good. (Well done if you guessed it.) Although sonsy, the last
Scottish word in this collection, is listed in all three of the dictionaries, I again
defer (in the first instance, at least) to Jamieson:[113]

1. Lucky; fortunate.
2. Good-humored; well-conditioned.
3. Having a pleasant look.
4. Plump; thriving.
5. Denoting fullness, conjoined with cordiality in the host.

And if that set of qualities isn't exemplary enough, the OED adds "sound,
sensible; shrewd," the RH2 adds "strong and healthy; robust," and the W3
adds "comfortably relaxed."

ᕱᕵ AGE

Early 16th century

ᕱᕵ ETYMOLOGY

Sonsy is an adaptation of the Gaelic *sonas*, "good fortune, prosperity." Its
antonym is the rhythmically compatible donsy, from the Gaelic *donas*, "bad
luck, misfortune."[114]

ᕱᕵ RARITY

Very rare

ᕱᕵ WHY I LIKE THE WORD SONSY

While Jamieson's definitions are not cumulative—a sonsy girl need not possess
all of the qualities simultaneously—it is interesting to ponder whether or not
any one earthly being *could* be so endowed. Such a person would certainly
epitomize the *summum bonum* of the quality of **kalon**.

But, given its heritage, the unsurprising reality is that sonsy is far from an elitist term and, as the OED notes, its qualities can be: "Of women or girls. Of the face. Of things. Of animals: Tractable, manageable."

Sonsy is, indeed, a versatile adjective, and one that I would aspire to earn if I were a girl, or a goat.

❧ SONSY ALIVE

Later that night Bill reopened the topic of rusticating, expanding on his desire to leave his job and do something different.

Jane listened carefully, then asked, "You're serious about this?"

Bill nodded, "I am."

"Right then, we'll need to talk it through properly, and we will. But now I have some other activities in mind."

Bill smiled and whispered to his beautiful wife, "Rosie may be Angelo's 'inamorata,' but you, Jane Mitchell, are my **sonsy** wife, and I love you."

sprezzatura

{sprətts-ah-TOO-rah. Noun.}

ᖇᔓ MEANING

The OED defines sprezzatura as: "Ease of manner, studied carelessness; the appearance of acting or being done without effort; spec. of literary style or performance."

Sprezzatura is not listed in either the RH2 or the W3 but, unexpectedly, it is in the *Merriam-Webster's Collegiate Dictionary, 11th Edition* (2003): "studied nonchalance: perfect conduct or performance of something (as an artistic endeavor) without apparent effort."

Wikipedia describes sprezzatura as "the art of making the difficult look easy."[116]

ᖇᔓ AGE

Mid-20th century

ᖇᔓ ETYMOLOGY

Sprezzatura is a loanword from Italian.

ᖇᔓ RARITY

Very rare

ᖇᔓ WHY I LIKE THE WORD SPREZZATURA

"Studied carelessness." What a delicious oxymoron!

Sprezzatura is what Maxwell Smart and Inspector Clousseau passionately desired but comically failed to achieve, and what Luciano Pavarotti embodied. And, I suspect, it is what Prince Charles has been trying his darnedest to pull off for years, with mixed results. Prince William, on the other hand, *had* sprezzatura, but I think it is waning as the seriousness of his position inexorably intensifies.

For me, I couldn't "do" sprezzatura if I tried day and night. I do care*ful*, I very occasionally do care*free*, but I don't think I'm capable of care*less*. But I find it fascinating that some people have the will and energy to affect unconcern. I get the whole cool, James Dean thing, but it must be tricky trying to determine when you need to *appear* unconcerned and when you can go back to just *being* unconcerned. I find it exhausting just to think about it.

That said, the sprezzatura achieved by great artists totally inspires and invigorates me. I have been very fortunate to be able to attend more than my fair share of live performances by musicians, actors, dancers, and other performance artists and, when an artist (or indeed an athlete) is able to achieve sprezzatura, it is a truly great achievement and, I think, a very precious gift to the audience.

ꙮ SPREZZATURA ALIVE

Jane met Rosamund and Angelo at the airport. It was a beautiful day and she was determined to just enjoy being with Rosamund and to not let Angelo's presence put her in a bad mood. She would even ignore his inane chatter, **sprezzatura**, and slightly overpowering cologne. This was a day for the sisters.

subsidiarity

{sub-sid-ee-AHR-ə-tee. Noun.}

ᴧᴑ MEANING

The OED defines subsidiarity as: "The quality of being subsidiary; specially the principle that a central authority should have a subsidiary function, performing only those tasks which cannot be performed effectively at a more immediate or local level."

Having performed a reasonable amount of work in the sustainability field, I know of numerous other definitions (including ones from the W3, Wikipedia and Wiktionary), but they all use different words to say the same thing so I will let the OED's perfectly accurate definition stand alone.

ᴧᴑ AGE

Mid-20th century

ᴧᴑ ETYMOLOGY

According to the OED, subsidiarity is a translation of the German *Subsidiarität*, whereas both the W3 and Wiktionary opt for "subsidiary" as its etymon. The OED lists subsidiary and the French *subsidiarité* as words to which one should "confer" (cf.).

ᴧᴑ RARITY

Rare

ᴧᴑ WHY I LIKE THE WORD SUBSIDIARITY

I have chosen this term for the simple reason that I think it is an important one that more of us should know.

We live at a time unlike any other. The fossil record tells us that humans (*Homo sapiens*) have been around for at least 130,000 years,[118] and yet our population only reached one billion in 1804. Staggeringly, we doubled that number in just 123 years (1927), added another billion 34 years later (1961), and a fourth 13 years after that (1974). We now number more than 6.6 billion and, while our rate of population growth has steadied,[119] our impact on our environment continues to increase exponentially. What this tells me is that we live in volatile conditions and that we should be wary of over-extending ourselves. I am thinking house of cards. I am thinking collapse.

So a principle like subsidiarity is wildly attractive to me and I feel passionately that it represents the kind of topic that we should be exercising our brain cells on, rather than, for example, how to make a quick buck "buying low and selling high."

In practical terms, subsidiarity simply means that we should seek to meet our needs locally and only divest responsibility further afield when it is truly beneficial. It doesn't mean that all national and international trade should stop tomorrow, and it certainly doesn't mean that we should put an end to all of the artistic, scientific, educational, social, and political collaboration that now takes place at a global level; but it does mean that the ideal of governance and sustainable trade absolutely must lie closer to home. As a society we dawdle for all things but the economy; for that we sprint. Subsidiarity tells us that we are sprinting in precisely the wrong direction.

∽ SUBSIDIARITY ALIVE

Subsidiarity! Bill finally remembered the word he had been trying to think of. The trigger had been an agreement he was working on for a subsidiary company to recycle more of the waste products from the company's plants. And that triggered another idea. Perhaps he could usefully employ his scientific and management knowledge to design a self-supporting, community-run, *local* recycling plant. After last night, Bill felt as if he could do anything.

tatum

{TAY-təm. Noun.}

MEANING

Tatum is a recently coined (1993) musical term that, I have no doubt, will soon find its way into the OED and other dictionaries.

The entry for tatum in Ohio State University's *Music Cognition Handbook: A Glossary of Concepts*[121] reads: "*Temporal atom*: the shortest duration in a notated musical work (or MIDI performance) that can be used as a divisor for all other durations. For example, if all nominal durations in a work are divisible into sixteenth durations, and the sixteenth duration is the largest such divisor, the sixteenth value is deemed the tatum for the work. The term *tatum* was coined at the Center for New Music and Audio Technologies at the University of California, Berkeley in 2000 [sic], and was named to evoke the rapid-fire piano playing of jazz keyboardist, Art Tatum."[122]

AGE

Late 20th century

ETYMOLOGY

As you can see from the quotation, tatum was coined by Jeff Bilmes in 1993. It appears from that quotation that tatum is, indeed, an eponym of the great jazz pianist Art Tatum (1909–1956), but it is not totally clear if its thoroughly apt connection to "temporal atom" was a simultaneous or subsequent event.

Well, you know what they say about the horse's mouth. I e-mailed Jeff Bilmes (who is now an Associate Professor at the University of Washington) to seek clarification and he kindly obliged. "I chose the word 'tatum' and I chose that particular spelling specifically to honor Art Tatum, but also because of the similarity to [Barry Vercoe's] 'temporal atom' which could be shortened to 'tatom'. . . . The association of the word tatum with 'temporal atom' and Art Tatum was simultaneous."

How about them apples!

RARITY

Extremely rare

❧ WHY I LIKE THE WORD TATUM

When I discovered tatum I had no idea of its fascinating etymology—I was simply interested in its meaning, particularly in how humans are able to perceive something intangible such as a beat. But digging around has led me to the breathtaking music of Art Tatum. "Rapid-fire piano playing" is no exaggeration—you could even call the notes **plesiosynchronous**!

I have also had the satisfaction of solving an etymological puzzle. Having been put off the scent by the OSU glossary's reference to tatum being coined in 2000, I eventually found an online poster from a 1996 UC Berkeley web page[126] advertising a project by the CNMAT Rhythm Research Group, of which Jeff Bilmes was a member. This led me to the quotation and thence to Jeff.

One last thought: What should the plural be? Despite the subject of the message in the quotation, it follows that, as the name is an eponym, the plural should be tatums. After all, you wouldn't call Mr. and Mrs. Tatum (Art was married twice, incidentally) "the Tata."

❧ TATUM ALIVE

Jerry, a musician in his spare time, had introduced Bill to a new word today—**tatum**—and it immediately made Bill wonder if there was a word for the shortest amount of time between money being earned and being spent. Clearly, this unit of measure would have to extend to negative values.

thalweg

{TAL-vehg. Noun.}

MEANING

The RH2 defines a thalweg (note the pronunciation) as:

1. A line, as drawn on a map, connecting the lowest points of a valley.
2. *Chiefly International Law.* The middle of the main navigable channel of a waterway that serves as a boundary line between states.

The W3's listing has two comparable definitions, the first noting that the "line following the lowest part of a valley" is a thalweg "whether under water or not." This is significant because, otherwise, where does the valley "line" stop and the river "line" start? The OED doesn't spell out this important transition, but rather implies it: "The line in the bottom of a valley in which the slopes of the two sides meet, and which forms a natural watercourse; also the line following the deepest part of the bed or channel of a river or lake." Note that rather than the river line being "the middle of the main navigable channel," the OED's definition places it at "the deepest part of the bed or channel." I imagine this sometimes makes a significant difference to where "a boundary line" is situated.

AGE

Early 19th century

ETYMOLOGY

From the German *thalweg*, "bottom path of a valley," from *thal*, "valley," and *weg*, "way."

RARITY

Rare

WHY I LIKE THE WORD THALWEG

I love geography and maps and this word simply brings the lines on maps to life. I am pretty sure that, if I have ever wondered where a border lay on a river, I would have assumed it was right down the middle. But it makes sense that

> If the boundary be taken to be the geographical center, the result will be a crooked line, conforming to the indentations and windings of the coast, but without relation to the needs of shipping. Minnesota v. Wisconsin, supra. If the boundary be taken to be the **thalweg**, it will follow the course furrowed by the vessels of the world.
>
> **U.S. Supreme Court**
> *New Jersey v. Delaware*, 291 U.S. 361 (1934)[127]

it should be down the middle of the main navigable channel so the channel is not "owned," or controlled, by either party.

Another reason this word caught my attention relates to the point where the valley's thalweg meets the river's thalweg. In his superb book, *A Short History of Progress* (Text Publishing Company, 2004), Canadian "historical philosopher" (I love the title, and it is quite appropriate) Ronald Wright uses the example of "the ornate Mayan city of Copan" to illustrate one of the many ways that cities collapse. He describes how, like so many other settlements around the world, this city "began as a small village on good bottom land beside a river"—that is, adjacent to where the dry thalweg and wet thalweg meet. Cue, then, what he aptly calls "a progress trap": "But as [the city] grew, it paved over more and more of its best land. Farmers were driven onto fragile hillside soils whose anchoring timber had been cleared. As the city died, so much silt washed down that whole houses and streets were buried."[128] And how many times has this process been repeated in human history?

◌ THALWEG ALIVE

As an interior designer, Jane seldom saw anything really "new" when it came to homeware, but today she saw something she just had to have. It was a tea-green colored, snowshoe-shaped bowl in the form of what the shop assistant told Jane was the base of a New Zealand nikau palm frond. Where the snowshoe tail would be was the cut-off stem of the frond, which acted as a kind of handle with a **thalweg** running down the middle of it and falling away into the bowl proper. It was so unusual and so beautiful that Jane bought one for herself, and one for Rosamund, too.

tramontane

{trah-MON-tayn. Adjective and noun.}

ᕔ MEANING

This is a rich word, both as an adjective (which can also be spelled **transmontane**) and as a noun. The RH2's entry has seven definitions, the first four for the adjective and the rest for the noun:

1. Being or situated beyond the mountains.
2. Beyond the Alps as viewed from Italy; transalpine.
3. Of, pertaining to, or coming from the other side of the mountains.
4. Foreign; barbarous.
5. A person who lives beyond the mountains: formerly applied by the Italians to the peoples beyond the Alps, and by the latter to the Italians.
6. A foreigner; outlander; barbarian.
7. A violent, polar wind from the northwest that blows in southern France.

ᕔ AGE

Late 16th century

ᕔ ETYMOLOGY

From the Italian *tramontana*, "north wind, pole-star," from the Latin *transmontanus*, "beyond the mountains."

ᕔ RARITY

Very rare

ᕔ WHY I LIKE THE WORD TRAMONTANE

New Zealand's capital city, Wellington, has something of a reputation as "the windy city." Having lived there for three years I can categorically confirm that the monicker fits, but "tramontane" has shown me that being "wind-centric" may involve rather more than anything I have experienced as a temporary Wellingtonian.

Indeed, in Wellington they talk about the southerly (being the cold wind) and the northerly or nor'easter (being the warm wind), and that's about it. But in Mediterranean countries bordering the Alps there are names for the winds that blow from every point on the compass. The famous mistral wind blows in from the northwest and is tramontane's immediate westerly neighbor. But there are six more winds, from the zephyrus (blowing in from the west) all the way round to the gregale (blowing in from the northeast).[129]

So the RH2's seventh definition was of great interest to me, but to get to it I had to traverse alpine mountains and negotiate my way past barbarians and even "outlanders." I love the imagery and primalism of this word—what else comes from "beyond the mountains"? Whatever it is, it must be "foreign" and "barbarous," because . . . well, because it's unknown, I guess.

I love the idea of scary tramontane visitors (like British football supporters descending on AC Milan's San Siro Stadium) and I love the fact that, to the Italians (and the Swiss, the Germans, the Austrians and who knows who else), the French are all tramontanes, just as the Italians themselves are tramontanes to all those east, north and west of the Alps. It seems to me to be name-calling of the most **desipient** order, and I just hope the opportunity arises when I can have a turn.

❧ TRAMONTANE ALIVE

So the **tramontane** couple had returned to dreary old London and now, Bill wondered, what was next? By all accounts Angelo's London practice continued to be a cash cow so Angelo would be sure to become restless again, and sooner rather than later. Bill felt strongly that Rosamund's life had been disrupted enough by Angelo's constant upheavals but, distressingly, he just didn't know how to prevent it from happening again.

trilemma

{try-LEMM-mah. Noun.}

❧ MEANING

A trilemma, according to the OED, is simply "a situation . . . of the nature of a dilemma, but involving three alternatives instead of two." The OED's definition of a dilemma, at least of its "popular use," is: "A choice between two (or, loosely, several) alternatives, which are or appear equally unfavorable; a position of doubt or perplexity, a 'fix.'"

The plural noun is **trilemmas** or **trilemmata**.

❧ AGE

Late 17th century

❧ ETYMOLOGY

Formed after "dilemma" (which is adopted from the Greek *dilemma*, "double proposition" from *di-*, "two, twice," and *lemma*, "assumption, premise," via Latin) from *tri-*, "three, thrice," and *lemma*.

❧ RARITY

Rare

❧ WHY I LIKE THE WORD TRILEMMA

A trilemma is exponentially more perplexing than a dilemma. Instead of just choosing from option A or B, you have option A, B, or C and the combined effect of *not* choosing A and B, A and C, or B and C. Put another way, instead of choosing between the lesser of two evils, you are choosing between the lesser of six evils.

Living with three very different females, I eat trilemmas for breakfast, but I won't bore you with my trivial conundrums. Let's jump straight to a trilemma that is so thorny it has its own name, Epicurus's Trilemma. The context is the logic of the Greek philosopher Epicurus (who equated good with pleasure and bad with pain, and who was probably an **ataraxic**) and his dissatisfaction with God (or any god, I presume) being labeled as either omnipotent or omnibenevolent.

1. If God is willing but unable to prevent evil, he is not omnipotent.
2. If God is able but not willing to prevent evil, he is not good.
3. If God is willing and able to prevent evil, then why is there evil?[131]

So, if we accept Epicurus's logic, we then have to decide whether we think God is weak, bad or uncaring. Or find a fourth option—but then we could just end up with a polylemma (yes, it's a real word).

I perhaps should have mentioned earlier that the Wikipedia article for trilemma also offers (rather optimistically, I think) a different interpretation of the definition: "There are two logically equivalent ways in which to express a trilemma: it can be expressed as a choice among three unfavorable options, one of which must be chosen, or as a choice among three favorable options, only two of which are possible at the same time."[132]

I don't think there are any famous trilemmas of the latter variety and, in any case, isn't that just being spoiled for choice?

❧ TRILEMMA ALIVE

Although Jane was excited about having Rosamund back in London (though not next door, since Mr. Addison had a 12-month lease, and, anyway, Rosamund's house would never be salubrious enough for Angelo), Jane's thoughts were dominated by her diligent consideration of the lifestyle **trilemma** Bill had discussed: escalate, hold steady, or change. So far, Jane had only got as far as working out that escalation was the true default—they hadn't held anything steady in years.

tu quoque

{t(y)oo-KWOH-kwee or too-KWOH-kway. Noun and adjective.}

❧ MEANING

The OED defines tu quoque as "an argument which consists in retorting a charge upon one's accuser."

Untypically, the RH2 defines it more formally as: "*Latin.* thou too: a retort by one charged with a crime accusing an opponent who has brought the charges of a similar crime."

❧ AGE

Early 17th century

❧ ETYMOLOGY

From the Latin *tu quoque*, "you also" or "thou too."

❧ RARITY

Very rare

❧ WHY I LIKE THE PHRASE TU QUOQUE

Just as a respectful "touché" is more elegant than, "nice one, you got me," I think "tu quoque" is so much more elegant than, "oh yeah, and *you* can talk."

In the world of arguments, there will always be pots calling kettles black because we are all so alike; the actions that annoy us are similar, and the actions we perform (that annoy those around us) are equally similar.

Tu quoque arguments are a type of argument termed *argumentum ad hominem*, "argument against the man"; that is, against the arguer rather than whatever the argument is about.

In a court of law, every time a lawyer attacks the credibility of a witness, this is an instance of an ad hominem argument. If the witness can be proved to have ulterior motives for his or her "version of events," and be proved to have lied in similar situations, then this approach can beneficially spawn a new proposition: that the witness is not credible. But it is a logical fallacy to argue that any particular fact that the witness has stated is false merely because of the witness's character.

An ad hominem tu quoque specifically refers to "a claim that the person making the argument has spoken or acted in a way inconsistent with the argument."[133] In a "you-too" version, this means that if I criticize behavior "A," you then point out that I am also guilty of "A" and that, therefore, my criticism should be dismissed. In an "inconsistency" version, this means that if I claim "A," but you know that I once claimed something inconsistent with "A," then "A" is false.

Both of these arguments are logical fallacies: the conclusions don't follow from the premises. This doesn't mean that all tu quoque arguments are without merit—a person's past actions are often highly relevant to correctly judging their current actions—but being aware of their limitations can only be useful.

And, as for the ambiguous pronunciation—tu quo*kwee* or tu quo*kway*—my default is the *kwee* version, based simply on the fact that it is the only variant listed by both the OED and the W3.

⤜ TU QUOQUE ALIVE

Jane confided her lifestyle deliberations to Rosamund, and received an unexpected response.

"**Tu quoque**, Jane, you're just as muddled as I am!"

"Tu quoque? What does that mean?" Jane was confused.

"It means 'you too,' and it's one of the terms I've have learned since I started studying law."

Now Jane was completely confused, "You're studying law? Since when?"

"Since Angelo. He always has contracts to deal with so I just started helping out and one thing led to another and—actually, Jane, I'm not feeling muddled at all. This is the happiest and strongest that I've felt in years."

ubiety

{yoo-BAI-ə-tee. Noun.}

✿ MEANING

The OED's definition for this term is simply "condition in respect of place or location; local relationship; whereness," which seems a little imprecise when you compare it to the RH2's: "the property of having a definite location at any given time; state of existing and being localized in space."

The W3's definition is more akin to the RH2's and includes this important addition: "the abstract quality of being in position." You could perhaps argue that "whereness" incorporates that meaning, but I think spelling it out is helpful.

The adjective is **ubietous**.

✿ AGE

Late 17th century

✿ ETYMOLOGY

From the Latin *ubi*, "where," and the suffix -ety, a variant of -ity, which expresses state or condition.

✿ RARITY

Very rare

✿ WHY I LIKE THE WORD UBIETY

In an increasingly "connected" world, I don't think that we can ignore the fact that our digital ubiquity ("being everywhere at once") has led directly to dislocation and a paralyzing sense of nullibiety ("being nowhere") and liminality ("being neither here nor there").

Ubiety is an antidote to this dislocation.

Let me paint a very pleasant picture of ubiety. I am on a train traveling from Bonn to Munich. It is late summer. My traveling companion and I have a table to ourselves and on that table is a stick of French bread, soft cheese, garlicky German salami, a penknife, drinks, a European travel guidebook, a European map, our cameras, a William Horwood novel, my companion's diary, and a few pens. That's it. No laptop. No cellphone. No way to contact anyone, or to be contacted by anyone. No way to Google anything. No way to be anywhere but precisely *there*.

When we talk of giving someone our "undivided attention," this seems to me to be a sure sign that, while our attention at that moment may be focused on the other person, our own "focus" is on a world so much larger than the one we physically occupy. Within this much smaller world, as far as I can tell, we find most of the really good stuff of life: family, friends, community, contribution, tradition, wealth, sustainability, survival. Big dreams require focus and fertilization, not diffused energy and ubiquity. Ubiety makes everything we experience richer, sharper, and more sustaining, and that translates to a bounty of both imaginings and the capabilities needed to make them come true.

ꝥ UBIETY ALIVE

Jane left Rosamund's new apartment realizing that, perhaps for the first time since their parents died, she wasn't anxious for her sister. That just left herself to worry about and, when she really thought about it, she had to admit that she was stale. Perhaps Bill was right and they really did need substance, **ubiety**, and a roll-your-sleeves-up challenge that would enable them to see themselves front-and-center, rather than in the background of their frantic, domineering lifestyles.

velleity

{və-LEE-ə-tee. Noun.}

ᴄᴥ MEANING
From the OED:

1. The fact or quality of merely willing, wishing, or desiring, without any effort or advance towards action or realization.
2. With *a* and in the plural. A mere wish, desire, or inclination without accompanying action or effort.

The RH2's definition adds another nuance: "volition in its weakest form." Velleity is the very benchmark of caring minimally.

The adjective is **velleitous**.

ᴄᴥ AGE
Early 17th century

ᴄᴥ ETYMOLOGY
From the Latin *velleitas*, from *velle*, "to will, to wish, to be willing," and *-itas*, -ity.

ᴄᴥ RARITY
Very rare

ᴄᴥ WHY I LIKE THE WORD VELLEITY
Velleity is the word whose (and I quote myself, which is a little weird) "utter relevance, archaic age (around 400 years old) and extreme rarity immediately struck me as something special."

I cannot imagine that there are too many other English words that so accurately describe such a pervasive condition. I mean, sure, we have many words and phrases at our disposal to express that we don't care at all (don't give a damn, indifference), that we do care (love, passion, calling), and even that we secretly care but want to inflict a little pain by claiming that we don't (couldn't care less). But what about when we give just a little damn—not enough to

The ease of her words, the control of them, was meant to convey to Compton that her wish to know of her real parents was hardly more than a **velleity**, a thought that would come to one while watering a plant or peeling an orange.

Thomas Savage, *I Heard My Sister Speak My Name*
(Little, Brown, 1977)[135]

do anything about our limited interest or concern—but a totally unhelpful inkling of a damn all the same?

And everywhere you look you will find velleitous inklings of concern. For example, the velleitous concern for air quality and global warming displayed by the drivers of gas-guzzling, smoke-belching SUVs (and that stands for Sport Utility Vehicle, in case you have ever had a velleitous desire to look it up, but never got round to it).

I am convinced that velleity permeates our lukewarm blood and that talking about the condition and using the word will only help us to better recognize our own behavior.

Let's resurrect this word.

⌒ VELLEITY ALIVE

Jane had reached a conclusion and it was time to tell Bill. "Let's do it," she said.

Bill was simultaneously excited, scared, worried and skeptical. "But what about your work? Your shops?"

Jane looked regretful, but only for a second. "I can commute. I can do select projects. Hey, I could even project-manage other designers. We'll find a way. Look, Bill, I've spent my life complaining about the velleitous folk who only talk the talk. I need to expel a little **velleity** of my own and just support *us*."

verbigerate

{ver-BIDJ-ə-reht. Verb.}

❧ MEANING

According to the W3, to verbigerate simply means "to repeat a word or sentence endlessly and meaninglessly." The OED categorizes the verb as a pathological term and defines it as meaning "to go on repeating the same word or phrase in a meaningless fashion, as a symptom of mental disease."

❧ AGE

Late 19th century

❧ ETYMOLOGY

From the Latin *verbigeratus*, from *verbigerare*, "to talk," from *verbum*, "word" and the suffix *gerare* (from the verb *gerere*, "to conduct, to carry").

❧ RARITY

Extremely rare

❧ WHY I LIKE THE WORD VERBIGERATE

I know I am preaching to the converted, but I will nevertheless take this very public opportunity to emphatically state to all those who suffer from non-clinical verbigeration, that talk is already cheap enough.

I am sure it has been well documented by sociolinguists and others that popular television programs such as *Beverly Hills 90210* were responsible, in the 1990s, for the rampant export of "like" from southern California to the world. Whether other English-speaking communities already did something similar is irrelevant, the global media machine was now involved and within a couple of years almost every teenage English speaker (as a first or second language) in the world had been "exposed."

It was also irrelevant that this particular fad had (and still has) no redeeming qualities; all that mattered was that the kids on the TV show said "like" all the time and that they were cool and that was enough, is enough and, I suspect, will always be enough. Moreover, this fad was (and continues to be) super-powered by the fact that its most ardent followers, teenage girls, love to talk.

It's like giving every teenage boy a Subaru *and* a gas card.

So that's *how* it happened, but what does it mean? I think assumptions by non-verbigerators that verbigerators are all "stupid," and assumptions by verbigerators that their verbigeration "doesn't matter" are equally inaccurate and unhelpful. Needlessly repeating the word "like" doesn't make you stupid but, like, you know, it like certainly makes you *appear*, like, stupid.

So, what can be done about it? If your kids are young enough, and you spend enough time with them, and they have teachers you can rely on, then maybe, just maybe, you can restrict enough of the flow of nutrients to the disease that it never quite takes hold. If, on the other hand, the horse has already bolted, then you could at least change the point of attack (if you haven't already) from verbigeration being something that you shouldn't do because it's immature and incorrect to being something that (and I'll roleplay here) "you know, you might decide for yourself that you don't want to do it because it makes *other* people think that you are stupid and immature. But, hey, you do whatever you think's best."

❧ VERBIGERATE ALIVE

It was just like the time when Bill and Jane got engaged: The brakes were off. They had a direction and a goal and they couldn't get enough of researching and planning. The last thing they wanted to do was go to a party hosted by Angelo but, for Rosamund's sake, they went.

It was a celebration for the friend of Angelo's who'd designed Rosamund's wedding dress. In two days' time the designer was holding her first official fashion show and, while this was great news for her, tonight it meant that a large number of people would have to endure hours on end of Angelo **verbigerating** about how her success was ultimately down to him.

veriloquent

{veh-RIL-oh-kwent. Adjective; also **veriloquous**.}

◈ MEANING

Veriloquent isn't in any of the three dictionaries, but the OED does list veriloquous as an obsolete adjective that means "speaking the truth; truthfulness, veracious." That entry also includes a note that veriloquent appeared in Thomas Blount's *Glossographia, or a dictionary interpreting such hard words . . . as are now used*, 1656.

The most recent dictionary listing for "veriloquent" that I can find is in the *Webster's Revised Unabridged Dictionary* (1913). Its definition is "speaking truth; truthful." This version of the adjective is also listed as obsolete.

The noun is **veriloquence**; the adverb is **veriloquently**.

◈ AGE

Mid-17th century

◈ ETYMOLOGY

My assumption is that veriloquent is derived from the Latin *verus*, "true," and *eloquent-is*, from *eloqui*, "to speak out."

◈ RARITY

Extremely rare

◈ WHY I LIKE THE WORD VERILOQUENT

No wonder this word is obsolete—speaking truthfully is something we humans are programmed *not* to do. This is why that famous Latin maxim is *in vino veritas* and not *in aqua veritas*—we have to be **bleezed**, that is, mind-altered, before we stop modifying reality with almost every breath.

Jim Carrey's character in the movie *Liar Liar* vividly illustrates the kind of bother we could all get into if we only ever spoke veriloquently. (And I think they actually played it rather tamely.) Oh, just imagine the consequences of veriloquence: *How do I look? Did you enjoy my lasagna? Would you like me to play you another song? Is that your best price?*

The truth is a scary thing, but I still aspire to speak it. And the noun veriloquence certainly has a grand sound to my ear—I would like to hear it uttered by others.

And, I have discovered, there are many other "loquences" that sound grand to my ear, and many that don't. In *There's a Word for It!* (Scribner, 2004), the self-confessed logomaniac ("a person obsessed with words") Charles Harrington Elster lists 26 ways to "speak out."[136] I will just tell you about a few of my favorites, but I do recommend you take a look at the full list in Charles's book.

First, I am a big fan of plain old eloquence, "the practice or art of using language with fluency and aptness" (RH2). Second, if we have to lie, we should at least lie mendaciloquently, that is, "artfully." And third, a pauciloquent speech—one "that uses few words" (OED, Draft Revision June 2005)—is always preferable to a longiloquent one (and I am assuming that word requires no definition).

୬ VERILOQUENT ALIVE

Bill was starting to wonder if a **veriloquent** sentence would ever pass Angelo's lips when he was rescued (or, rather, abducted) by a tremendously excited Jane who, without a word of explanation, dragged him by the arm until they were out of anyone's earshot. Then she whispered to him: "Rosamund just told me she is going to leave Angelo."

vibrissae

{vai-BRIS-ee. Plural noun.}

ᐅ MEANING

The W3 defines (with unusual detail[137]) the singular **vibrissa** as:

1. One of the stiff hairs that grow about the nostrils or on other parts of the face in many mammals (as the whiskers of a cat or the hairs of the nostrils of man) and that are not themselves sensitive but often serve as tactile organs; also: a similar stiff tactile hair growing elsewhere on some mammals (as in a small tuft at the wrist).
2. One of the feathers that resemble bristles near the mouth of many birds and especially of some insectivorous birds and that may help to prevent the escape of insects.

The singular noun is **vibrissa**.

ᐅ AGE

Late 17th century

ᐅ ETYMOLOGY

From the Latin *vibrissare*, "vibrant," from *vibrare*, "to shake, to vibrate." Vibrissae is cognate with words such as vibrant, vibration and vibrato.

ᐅ RARITY

Rare

ᐅ WHY I LIKE THE WORD VIBRISSAE

I chose this word for two reasons, one official and one unofficial.

Unofficially, I chose vibrissae for my cat.

Having two daughters and no other children means that, around my house, male company is in short supply. Simpson, the cat, is a boy, and we are simpatico; we are amigos. He lies on my desk for hours on end, his vibrissae twitching every time I move the computer mouse. I know he hangs out with me partly for the company, but mainly just for the relative peace and quiet of my desk compared with the rest of the house (which is all under feminine control).

So, forgive me, I had to find a word for my "son."

Now, the official reason I chose vibrissae is that it completes an important set. You probably haven't noticed that there has been a word in my list that directly relates to each of the five senses, except touch. For taste we had **ambrosia**, for sound we had **chavish**, for sight we had **glandaceous** and for smell we had **petrichor**.

As Charles Darwin wrote in *The Descent of Man*, "vibrissae . . . are used as organs of touch,"[138] which explains why Simpson can catch mice, rats, birds, and even a rabbit (once) at night. Interestingly, vibrissae (*not* "whiskers"— see the quotation) don't actually have nerves running through their length. Rather, they work by being rooted in tiny pockets of blood that are walled with sensors that tell the brain simple stuff such as: where the blood has moved and, therefore, which way the vibrissa has just moved and, therefore, the relative position and velocity of both the cat's head and whatever the vibrissa just rubbed against. Brilliant!

❧ VIBRISSAE ALIVE

Angelo's tall stories couldn't be halted, but Bill no longer cared. Angelo had moved on from his prowess as a launcher of artistic careers to his prowess as a hunter of bears. "I was so close, you know?"

Bill, deadpan: "I suppose you could see the bear's *teeth*."

"Teeth? Of course, the teeth, the teeth, but more. I was so close I could see his **vibrissae** twitching."

yoctosecond

{YOK-toh-sek-ənd. Noun.}

ᑤ MEANING
One septillionth of a second.
   The abbreviation is **ysec** or **ys**.

ᑤ AGE
Late 20th century

ᑤ ETYMOLOGY
From the International System of Units (SI) prefix *yocto-*, "denoting a factor of 10^{-24}," and second. According to the Wikipedia article on yocto-, it is (as of 2007) the smallest SI unit and was adopted in 1991. The prefix is derived from the Greek *octö-*, "eight," because it is $1/1000^8$.[139]

   It is interesting to note that even though "yoctosecond" is a new word, it is not a neologism, at least, not according to the W3 whose definition of a neologism—"a new word, usage, or expression"—is illustrated with and modified by this short but important quotation from R. A. Hall: "All neologisms begin as slang, except in those branches of terminology where . . . there is an established tradition of word coinage or redefinition." I would say the International System of Units has a fairly well-established tradition of coining words.

ᑤ RARITY
Extremely rare

ᑤ WHY I LIKE THE WORD YOCTOSECOND
Okay, so we have all heard of a millisecond—one thousandth of a second—and most of us might be able to guess the meaning of a microsecond (one millionth of a second) and have probably at least heard of a nanosecond (one billionth of a second). But did you realize that these fractions of time just keep getting smaller, to picosecond (one trillionth of a second), femtosecond (one quadrillionth of a second), attosecond (one quintillionth of a second), zeptosecond (one sextillionth of a second), and finally (for now), yoctosecond. And what does

one septillionth actually look like? Well it can look like this: 1,000,000,000, 000,000,000,000,000th, or like this: 0.000000000000000000000001. It's a very, very, very small fraction.

Now, I don't mind admitting that picosecond doesn't come up much in my work, but it must be a useful term to a great many people because it and femtosecond merely rate (by the standards of this book) as "rare," with only attosecond "very rare," and just zeptosecond joining yoctosecond as "extremely rare." And nanosecond? That wouldn't rate as "rare" at all.

But yoctosecond *is* "extremely rare"—it is an extremity of science—and how would you or I ever use this unit of time in any context other than as an item of trivia? Even the shortest possible **tatum** (presumably around 1/32nd of a beat) would be measured in milliseconds. Well, the great thing about this highly specialized term is that really only half of it is uncommon—the "yocto-" part. And the practice of placing a prefix in front of "second" to make it into a fraction of a second is common, hence millisecond. So I say we just go ahead and use this word for a little exaggeration here and there—I am sure others will get the idea *pronto pronto*.

☙ YOCTOSECOND ALIVE

Just when Bill was starting to wonder if he could survive another **yoctosecond** of Angeloisms, he received the blessed and long anticipated nod from Jane that it was time to go home. They quickly said their thank yous and *buona nottes* and left, both wondering if they would see Angelo again.

zaftig

{ZAFF-təg. Adjective; also **zoftick**, **zoftig**, **zoftik**.}

❧ MEANING

The OED lists zaftig as an American colloquialism meaning: "Of a woman: plump, curvaceous, 'sexy.'"

The quotation marks around the word "sexy" imply non-standard usage, but I am not sure such a thing is possible. Surely the meaning of "sexy" is inherently subjective and, therefore, inherently non-standard.

In any case, the American W3 and RH2 dictionaries leave no doubt about zaftig's connotations, with their definitions including the unequivocally positive "pleasingly plump" and "pleasantly plump," respectively.

❧ AGE

Mid-20th century

❧ ETYMOLOGY

Zaftig is a Yiddish[141] adoption of the German *saftig*, "juicy."

Wordsmith Anu Garg fondly describes Yiddish as "a tongue full of wit and charm [that] embodies deep appreciation of human behavior in all its colorful manifestations," and the language has certainly gifted us many wonderful words, particularly ones for cheekily describing those around us. How about these irreverent and poetic all-stars: schmuck ("an idiot"), kvetch ("a whiner"), schlimazel ("a born loser") and luftmensch ("a dreamer"—literally, "airman").

❧ RARITY

Rare

❧ WHY I LIKE THE WORD ZAFTIG

While I am a passionate proponent of respectfulness, there are many forms of what we now call political correctness of which I am not in favor. I think it is wiser to take a broader view of what is good or bad, better or worse, than simply the unquestioned fashion of the day.

A skinny woman is, at present, widely accepted as being physically "superior" to a woman with a fuller figure. Clearly this hasn't always been so

⚭ QUOTATION ⚭

Jasmine March, the **zaftig** heroine of this wickedly funny first novel, is a Washington cookbook writer who pines for the days of Louis XIV, "when men were gluttons and proud of it."

Jennifer Reese, "The Joy of Cooking"
The New York Times, 15 Dec. 2002

and, clearly, it won't always be so. The youthfulness of the word zaftig (it was only coined in the 1930s) is a salient reminder of just how quickly fashions change.

As a term that celebrates a timeless human truth (that a curvaceous female body, as well as being attractive, is typically going to be healthy and capable of bearing a child), I reckon we are better off with zaftig as an active—rather than an archaic—word in our lexicon.

⚭ ZAFTIG ALIVE

In fact, Bill and Jane saw Angelo just 48 hours later at the fashion show. Between Rosamund running around making plans for her future as a single woman and Angelo merely running around as he always did, there had been no time for "the talk." So Bill and Jane had felt obliged to honor their promise to attend Angelo's friend's show.

"Tomorrow," Jane whispered to Bill as yet another wave of uniformly skinny models strode up the catwalk, "she's going to tell him tomorrow."

Bill nodded and promised to be on call if Rosamund needed help moving things, or even if she wanted him to be present. And then Bill purposefully took a good long look at the **zaftig** curves of his beautiful wife before reconsidering the angular figures of the androgynous waifs on stage. He was a lucky man.

zemblanity

{zem-BLAN-ə-tee. Noun.}

MEANING

"The opposite of serendipity, the faculty of making unhappy, unlucky and expected discoveries by design."[142] The inevitable discovery of what we would rather not know.

The adjective is **zemblanitous**.

AGE

Late 20th century

ETYMOLOGY

Zemblanity was coined by the mischievous Scottish novelist William Boyd for his 1998 novel *Armadillo*. And not only is the meaning of the word the opposite of serendipity (the accidental discovery of something fortunate), Boyd enriched the deal with an etymological opposite as well.

So what is the etymology of serendipity? I had always assumed it was related to serene, but no such link exists. (Serene is derived from the Latin *serenus*, which means "clear or unclouded," as in a clear sky or clear weather.) Serendipity is in fact derived from the Persian word for Sri Lanka (*Serendip*). It was coined in 1754 by a talented British earl, Horace Walpole, who would have viewed Sri Lanka as a particularly attractive destination—a warm and exotic paradise. So, in searching for the root of his new word, Boyd sought out a wholly different kind of island and came up with the Russian archipelago of Nova Zembla (*Novaya Zemlya*), a barren former nuclear testing ground in the middle of the icy Arctic Ocean.

RARITY

Extremely rare

WHY I LIKE THE WORD ZEMBLANITY

My tour of arresting rare words ends with the newest of the 100 selected words. I hope this wonderful word serves as a reminder that there is nothing to stop *you* from coining a word.[143] The measure, as always, is in the usage.

So is *zemblanity* worth using? I certainly think so. It describes perfectly the process I endure every 20th of the month as I review income and expenses, dreading the inevitable discovery that the income is lower than expected, and the expenses are higher. And is there a better word to describe the inevitable disappointment of discovering that the bus that you just missed was, in fact, your bus?

∞ ZEMBLANITY ALIVE

Rosamund had arranged to meet Angelo at a café for lunch so, as soon as he left that morning, she began to pack her things. When she came to the box containing her wedding dress she sat still for a moment and thought about what had been a turbulent but exciting and, ultimately, valuable year. She had learned something very important—that she deserved something better than her life with Angelo.

She decided to pop in to Angelo's friend's apartment before going to lunch, in order to return the wedding dress. It wouldn't be right to keep it, and she knew Angelo hadn't got around to paying for it. When Rosamund saw Angelo's car parked just around the corner from the designer's apartment, the connections in her mind were like a burst of machine-gun fire: if, then, then, then, then. And as she pushed open the unlocked front door, she knew that she would discover him *in flagrante* and herself in **zemblanity**.

 Epilogue

Words on a page are just that. My hope in writing this book is that the qualities of at least a few of these 100 words have made you nod and smile and share the word with others. That's what bringing words to life is all about.

And if you know of a rare word of the caliber of a "concinnity," a "proficuous," or a "velleity," please do share it with others. I also invite you to share the word with me via my website (www.nakedize.com) and I will make sure others can enjoy it too.

Finally, for those statistically-minded folk, here are a few interesting facts about the 100 selected words.

- There is only one monosyllabic word (**bleezed**).
- The three rarest words are **cryptoscopophilia**, **elozable**, and **omnistrain**.
- The three oldest words are **ambsace**, **concupiscible**, and **handsel**.
- The three most recently coined (not borrowed) words are **infonesia**, **nikhedonia**, and **zemblanity**.
- If the words were evenly distributed by initial letter, you would expect around four of each in a 100-word list. Instead, just four letters, "a," "c," "p," and "s" account for almost half of the words (with 14, 9, 18, and 7 words respectively). There are no words beginning with "w" or "x."
- Approximately two-thirds of the words are derived from either Greek (30) or Latin (37), with French (6), German (4), and Italian (4) the next most common source languages.

Further Reading

BOOKS

Bryson, Bill. (1990) *Mother Tongue: The English language*. Hamish Hamilton.

Dickson, Paul. (1992) *Dickson's Word Treasury: A connoisseur's collection of old and new, weird and wonderful, useful and outlandish words*. John Wiley & Sons.

Elster, Charles Harrington. (1996) *There's a Word for It!: A grandiloquent guide to life*. Scribner.

Games, Alex. (2006) *Balderdash & Piffle: English words and their curious origins*. BBC Books.

Garg, Anu and Garg, Suti. (2002) *A Word A Day: A romp through some of the most unusual and intriguing words in English*. John Wiley & Sons.

Garg, Anu. (2005) *Another Word A Day: An all-new romp through some of the most unusual and intriguing words in English*. John Wiley & Sons.

Manser, Martin H. and Pickering, David (Associate Editor). (2007) *Buttering Parsnips, Twocking Chavs: The secret life of the English language*. Weidenfeld & Nicolson.

Moore, Christopher J. (2004) *In Other Words: A language lover's guide to the most intriguing words around the world*. Walker & Company.

Quinion, Michael. (2006) *Gallimaufry: A hodgepodge of our vanishing vocabulary*. Oxford University Press.

WEB SITES

A Word A Day (by Anu Garg)
www.wordsmith.org

Ask Oxford
www.askoxford.com

Dictionary.com
dictionary.reference.com

Merriam-Webster Online
www.merriam-webster.com

The Oxford English Dictionary
www.oed.com

Verbatim (quarterly language magazine)
www.verbatimmag.com

The Vocabula Review (British online magazine)
www.vocabula.com

Wikipedia – The Free Encyclopedia
www.wikipedia.org

Wiktionary – The Free Dictionary
www.wiktionary.org

Word Information (etymology)
www.wordinfo.info

Wordcraft
www.wordcraft.infopop.cc

Wordie
www.wordie.org

World Wide Words (by Michael Quinion)
www.worldwidewords.org

Worthless Word for the Day (by Michael A. Fischer)
home.comcast.net/~wwftd/

 Endnotes

1   Bryson, Bill. (1990) *Mother Tongue*. Hamish Hamilton, p. 60.
2   **Astrobleme** is in both the RH2 and the W3, but not in the OED.
3   Google.com.
4   Luther Blissett is a multiple-use nom de plume adopted and shared by hundreds of artists and social activists; <http://en.wikipedia.org/wiki/Luther_Blissett_(nom_de_plume)>
5   <http://www.nettime.org/Lists-Archives/nettime-l-9804/msg00077.html>
6   WoW stands for World of Warcraft, a multi-player online role-playing game; <http://www.wowwiki.com/Holy_Light> (accessed 31 Dec. 2007).
7   <http://www.gutenberg.org/files/22120/22120-8.txt>
8   Moore, Christopher J. (2004) *In Other Words: A language lover's guide to the most intriguing words around the world*. Walker & Company.
9   OED.
10   <http://www.lavuelta.com/04/ingles/noticias/noticias19.asp?e=19>
11   <http://1828.mshaffer.com/d/word/antiscian>
12   <http://www.languagehat.com/archives/001804.php> (accessed 3 Jan. 2008).
13   <http://redbrickroadstudios.com/episodes/III/ep3.11rant.html> (accessed 3 Jan. 2008).
14   A review of *Creation of the Sacred: Tracks of Biology in Early Religions by Walter Burkert* (Harvard University Press, 1996).
15   Baldick, Christopher. (1996) *The Concise Oxford Dictionary of Literary Terms*. Oxford University Press.
16   <http://www.otters.co.za/vdome_infopage.htm> (accessed 3 Jan. 2008).
17   Translated by Charles Cotton, revised by William Carew Hazlett.
18   <http://www.heritage.nf.ca/dictionary/azindex/pages/152.html> (accessed 6 Jan. 2008).
19   <http://encarta.msn.com/dictionary_1861739760/ballicatter.html> (accessed 6 Jan. 2008).
20   And Supplement (1825). Revised 1879–87.
21   *Jamieson's Dictionary of the Scottish Language*, Abridged by John Johnston. A New Edition, Revised and Enlarged, by John Longmuir, AM, LLD (William P. Nimmo, 1867).
22   <http://www.authorsden.com/visit/viewpoetry.asp?id=201318>
23   Dickson, Paul. (1992) *Dickson's Word Treasury: A connoisseur's collection of old and new, weird and wonderful, useful and outlandish words*. John Wiley & Sons, Chapter 48.
24   <http://lambgoat.com/albums/view.aspx?id=1289>
25   <http://www.testriffic.com/poem/AlexINTJ/119953>
26   <http://www.sussexhistory.co.uk/sussex-dialect/sussex-dialect%20-%200126.htm>
27   <http://www.cyclingnews.com/results/2000/jul00/tdfrance00/stages/tdfrance00st1r.shtml>
28   *Jamieson's Dictionary of the Scottish Language* (1867).

29 <http://www.lib.ed.ac.uk/faqs/parqsdth.shtml#Encyclo14> (accessed 20 Dec. 2007).

30 <http://danielfranklingomez.com/blog/2007/01/04/chris-daughtry-reviewed/>

31 Originally published as a censored and serialized version by *The Graphic*, a British illustrated newspaper.

32 <http://www3.merriam-webster.com/opendictionary/newword_search. php?word=dr>

33 <http://soccerdad.baltiblogs.com/archives/2007/03/13/if_you_must_03132007. html>

34 This was a briefing for "the United States in Opposition" regarding a Supreme Court case where the families of two servicemen killed during a Navy-organized rafting trip were seeking that a decision barring them from suing the government be overturned. The brief argued that such a review was unwarranted because, unlike the servicemen in the case mentioned in the quotation, the servicemen killed on the rafting trip were on duty and service members cannot sue the government while they are working for it. Interesting stuff, particularly the final qualification.

35 <http://www.usdoj.gov/osg/briefs/2001/0responses/2001-0526.resp.html>

36 <http://www.poemsabout.com/poet/cesare-giraldo>

37 Farrar, Frederick W. (1873) *Families of Speech*, iv.

38 <http://database.obsidianfleet.net/wiki/index.php/Sulamid> (accessed 31 Dec. 2007).

39 <http://en.wiktionary.org/wiki/imbroglio> (accessed 17 Jan. 2008).

40 <http://www.goldsmiths.ac.uk/history/news-events/leibniz-paper.doc> via <http:// www.goldsmiths.ac.uk/history/news-events/working-papers.php> (accessed 4 Jan. 2008).

41 <http://www.covertcomic.com/CCSchool.htm>

42 <http://famousamericans.net/patrickhenryshields/>

43 Taylor, A. J. P. (1945) *The Course of German History*.

44 In *Ordered Profusion*.

45 <http://www.askoxford.com/asktheexperts/faq/aboutenglish/proportion?view=uk> (accessed 18 Dec. 2007).

46 <http://www.japan-101.com/culture/karoshi.htm>

47 <http://en.wikipedia.org/wiki/Karoshi> (accessed 10 Feb. 2008).

48 <http://www.the-triton.com/megayachtnews/index.php?news=823>

49 <http://lexin.nada.kth.se/lexin-en.html>

50 <http://en.wikipedia.org/wiki/Lagom>

51 Revised in 2007. See <http://www.johnalexander.se>

52 *The American Heritage Stedman's Medical Dictionary.* Houghton Mifflin Company. 12 Dec. 2007. <Dictionary.com http://dictionary.reference.com/browse/ lalochezia>

53 Published at the Centre for Cancer Education, University of Newcastle upon Tyne.

54 <http://www.infofaith.com/info/index.php?option=com_content&task= view&id=72&Itemid=36>

55 The full article is online at <http://www.oxfordstudent.com/tt2006wk2/Features/

not_so_queer_as_folk>. It is well worth reading if you enjoyed the appetizer.

56 <http://en.wikipedia.org/wiki/List_of_English_words_invented_by_Shakespeare> (accessed 19 Jan. 2008).
57 <http://www.impalapublications.com/blog/index.php?/archives/2005/12/11.html>
58 <http://lychnobiteas.co.uk/>
59 <http://en.wikipedia.org/wiki/Maieutics> (accessed 19 Jan. 2008).
60 First published in 1973. See <http://www.canedisanbernardo.org/engl/capitolo6bis-engl.html>
61 <http://en.wiktionary.org/wiki/millihelen> (accessed 20 Jan. 2008).
62 <http://en.wikipedia.org/wiki/List_of_humorous_units_of_measurement#_note-4> (accessed 20 Jan. 2008).
63 Obscure Words. © 2007 by Michael A. Fischer <http://home.comcast.net/~wwftd>.
64 <http://www.consortiumnews.com/2006/111306b.html>
65 <http://en.wikipedia.org/wiki/Sub_rosa> (accessed 7 Dec. 2007).
66   <http://www.wordinfo.info>
67 <http://www.wordinfo.info/words/index/info/view_unit/2502>
68 <http://en.wikipedia.org/wiki/Noosphere> (accessed 3 Jan. 2008).
69 <http://www.wired.com/wired/archive/4.05/net_surf.html>
70 <http://www.eo.ucar.edu/basics/wx_1_b.html>
71 <http://en.wikipedia.org/wiki/Omnism> (accessed 15 Dec. 2007).
72 The web site's "last updated" date.
73 Elster, Charles Harrington. (1996) *There's A Word For It!: A grandiloquent guide to life*. Scribner, p. 21.
74 I did discover that Omnistrain (with a capital O) is a Q-tronic trading card.
75 <http://yeshivabachur.blogspot.com/2005_06_01_archive.html>
76 <http://www.drbilllong.com/2006Words/Motins.html>
77 <http://en.wikipedia.org/wiki/Rhetoric_device> (accessed 21 Jan. 2008).
78 <http://www.jewishworldreview.com/cols/chavez120500.asp>
79 OED (Draft Revision Dec. 2007).
80 Ibid.
81 <http://en.wikipedia.org/wiki/Image:JohnHancockSignature.jpg>
82 <http://en.wikipedia.org/wiki/Image:Autograph_of_Elizabeth_I_of_England_%28from_Nordisk_familjebok%29.png>
83 OED (Draft Revision Dec. 2005).
84 OED (Draft Revision June 2007).
85 <http://www.pcguide.com/vb/archive/index.php/t-20906-p-3.html> (accessed 2 Jan. 2008).
86 <http://en.wikipedia.org/wiki/Petrichor> (accessed 24 Jan. 2008).
87 <http://en.wikipedia.org/wiki/Adsorb> (accessed 24 Jan. 2008).
88 OED.
89 <http://en.wikipedia.org/wiki/Philtrum> (accessed 24 Jan. 2008).
90 OED (Draft Revision Mar. 2006).
91 <http://www.choiceodds.com/faq/glossary/plesiosynchronous>

(accessed 1 Jan. 2008).

92 Byrne, J. F. (1953) *Silent Years*, xix. 247.

93 Quoted from "Lukomski on Cameron" (an online book), from the web site of the Alexander Palace Association. See <http://www.alexanderpalace.org/cameron/two. html> (accessed 4 Jan. 2008).

94 OED (Draft Entry June 2004).

95 <http://www.americandialect.org/index.php/amerdial/plutoed_voted_2006_ word_of_the_year/>

96 *The Examiner*, 337(1), 30 May 1824.

97 <http://home.comcast.net/~wwftd/pq.htm>

98 <http://en.wikipedia.org/wiki/Poshlost> (accessed 4 Jan. 2008).

99 Nabokov, Vladimir, *Nikolai Gogol* (*New Directions*, 1944).

100 Alexandrov, Vladimir. (1991) *Nabokov's Otherworld*. Princeton University Press, page 106.

101 Boym, Svetlana. (1994) *Common Places: Mythologies of Everyday Life in Russia*. Harvard University Press.

102 <http://www.long-sunday.net/long_sunday/2006/01/poshlost.html>

103 <http://en.wikipedia.org/wiki/D%C3%A9j%C3%A0_vu> (accessed 4 Jan. 2008).

104 <http://www.tactus.biz/store/product_info.php?manufacturers_ id=141&products_id=78&language=en&osCsid=d7>

105 <http://metabole.blogspot.com/2005/08/reify-imagination.html>

106 OED.

107 <http://www.redpepper.org.uk/article415.html>

108 <http://en.wikipedia.org/wiki/Saudade> (accessed 24 Dec. 2007).

109 The book was reissued in 2000 by Sarabande Books, Louisville, Kentucky.

110 <http://www.amazon.com/They-Have-Word-Howard-Rheingold/ dp/0874774640>

111 <http://www.jewishworldreview.com/cols/jonah080101.asp>

112 <http://www.neologophile.com/graffiti/index.php?entry=1123843626>

113 *Jamieson's Dictionary of the Scottish Language* (1867).

114 OED.

115 <http://thekaetlancaresnot.blogspot.com/2003/05/on-halloween-in-high-school-even.html>

116 <http://en.wikipedia.org/wiki/Sprezzatura> (accessed 29 Jan. 2008).

117 <http://www.fountainpennetwork.com/forum/index.php?s=b38d1af2649cce3f0d 2115d9416a039b&showtopic=42088&st=60&p=396073&#entry396073>

118 <http://anthropology.si.edu/humanorigins/ha/sap.htm>

119 <http://en.wikipedia.org/wiki/World_population> (accessed 29 Jan. 2008).

120 <http://www.mindhenge.co.uk/28june04.html>

121 By David Huron.

122 <http://www.music-cog.ohio-state.edu/Music838/glossary.html>

123 Bilmes, J. (1993) "Timing is of the Essence: Perceptual and Computational Techniques for Representing, Learning, and Reproducing Expressive Timing in

Percussive Rhythm," Master Thesis. MIT, Cambridge.

124 I assume the square brackets are Jim's (in both instances); the "sic" is mine (Art Tatum played the piano, not the drum).

125 <http://www.auditory.org/mhonarc/2002/msg00135.html>

126 <http://cnmat.berkeley.edu/Rhythm/poster.html>

127 <http://supreme.justia.com/us/291/361/case.html>

128 IV Pyramid Schemes, p. 100.

129 <http://en.wikipedia.org/wiki/Tramontane> (accessed 30 Jan. 2008).

130 <http://en.wikipedia.org/wiki/Trilemma> (accessed 2 Jan. 2008).

131 Ibid.

132 Ibid.

133 <http://en.wikipedia.org/wiki/Ad_hominem> (accessed 31 Jan. 2008).

134 <http://michaelgates.blogspot.com/2006_08_01_archive.html>. The quoted text by Craig Bell was published by Xlibris in 2002.

135 Republished as *The Sheep Queen* (Back Bay Books, 2001).

136 Chapter 9, pp. 195–7.

137 The W3 entry also lists a third definition regarding a pair of stout bristles on certain two-winged flies.

138 Darwin, Charles. (1871) *The Descent of Man*, Man I. i. 25.

139 <http://en.wikipedia.org/wiki/Yocto-> (accessed 31 Jan. 2008).

140 <http://homepage.mac.com/lymond/ew/C1592649901/E1480006283/index.html>

141 Yiddish (or Eastern Yiddish) is the non-territorial language of central and eastern European Jews and their descendants. It is a Germanic language (part of the Indo-European family) but its writing system is based on the Hebrew script. According to *Ethnologue*, Yiddish today has more than 3 million speakers spread across the globe—the largest communities being located in Israel and the United States.

142 Boyd, William. (1998) *Armadillo*. Knopf, Chapter 12.

143 I coined the verb nakedize—"to uncover a true goal; to reveal true motivation; to simplify; to unclutter"—in 2003, and then named my own company after it. So the word breathes, just. Will it ever force its way into a dictionary? Only time will tell.

144 <http://barbourblog.blogspot.com/2007/09/another-vision.html>

# Index

The words given in bold refer to full entries in the book.